BORDERLINE PERSONALITY DISORDER

A COMPREHENSIVE GUIDE TO TREAT AND MANAGE BPD!

By

DR MARIA GUHIVER

otherwise, by any usage or abuse of any policies, processes, or directions contained within is the solitary and utter responsibility of the recipient reader. Under no circumstances will any legal responsibility or blame be held against the publisher for any reparation, damages, or monetary loss due to the information herein, either directly or indirectly.

Respective authors own all copyrights not held by the publisher.

The information herein is offered for informational purposes solely, and is universal as so. The presentation of the information is without contract or any type of guarantee assurance.

The trademarks that are used are without any consent, and the publication of the trademark is without permission or backing by the trademark owner. All trademarks and brands within this book are for clarifying purposes only and are the owned by the owners themselves, not affiliated with this document

Table of Contents

INTRODUCTION

Borderline personality Disorder signifies a disturbance in a typical personality feature that is manifested through personality as well as mood instability. It could simply be that your unfavorable life mirrors the experiences of a person with the condition. Borderline personality condition is treatable with a series of psychiatric therapy and suggested medicines.

The start of borderline personality condition symptoms generally occurs during the duration of the teenage years. To make sure accuracy, the diagnosis and therapy of personality conditions are often postponed until the period of maturity. Medical professionals find it essential to discount the impact of personality advancement on behavior issues before jumping to any conclusion.

The specific causes of Borderline Personality Condition vary from individual to individual, yet at its very core, the impacts are comparable. The majority of individuals with Borderline Personality Condition aren't fast to seek out treatment on their very own, but with the right motivation, it can be helped.

What Actually Triggers BPD?

As mentioned above, there is no one 'main' cause when it comes to Borderline Personality Disorder. It can be something deeply rooted in our brain's structure or chemistry can sadly be an item of condition. Youth issues, misuse, desertion, and so on, can all bring about concerns with BPD. Several of the problems do not appear until later on in life, which can be confusing in diagnosis. One of the most important things, however, is to recognize the symptoms of BPD, which can be various on an instance by situation basis.

What Are Some Symptoms To Seek?

Despite the fact that every person responds to BPD in a different way, it is necessary to understand signs before they end up being too major to manage, as well as the person struggling, can injure themselves or someone else. Some typical symptoms consist of:

A feeling of solitude or emptiness

Fear of being alone

Impulsive behavior (particularly in connections, with funds, and so on).

Unwarranted anger.

Dullness.

Addiction/Self-Harm.

These signs can bring about a risky way of living in many circumstances, making this condition exceptionally harmful for the person entailed, and also those around them. Due to the fact that lots of people dealing with BPD hate being alone, they'll additionally be quick to jump from partnership to relationship - one more instance of impulsive habits and also choices. Not just is this harmful for them as an individual, yet it can be easy for a person to benefit from that kind of habits.

Characteristics

People with Borderline Character Disorder make agitated initiatives to stay clear of genuine or pictured desertion. The assumption of putting at risk separation or being rejected, or the loss of exterior framework, can lead to extensive changes in self-image, affect, cognition, as well as habits. Their agitated initiatives to prevent abandonment may include spontaneous actions such as suicidal or self-mutilating actions.

Individuals with Borderline Personality Disorder have a pattern of intense and also unsteady connections. These individuals can understand with and also nurture various other people, however only with the expectation that the other person will "be there" in return to meet their own requirements on demand. These individuals are susceptible to significant as well as unexpected shifts in their sight of others, which might alternately be seen as beneficent supports or as cruelly punishing.

There may be an identity disruption characterized by markedly and also persistently unsteady self-image or feeling of self. There are remarkable and also abrupt changes in self-image, defined by moving goals, worths, and occupation aspirations. There might be sudden changes in opinions as well as plans concerning career, sex-related identification, values, as well as types of friends. These individuals may all of a sudden transform from the duty of a clingy supplicant for aid to an exemplary avenger of past mistreatment. Although they usually have a self-image that is based upon being negative or wicked, people with this condition might, at times, have felt that they do not exist whatsoever. Such experiences normally take place in scenarios in which the private feel an absence of a significant relationship, nurturing, as well as support. These individuals may show worse performance in disorganized job or institution situations.

People with Borderline Personality Disorder present impulsivity in at the very least 2 locations that are possibly self-damaging. They may gamble, invest money irresponsibly, binge eat, abuse materials, participate in unsafe sex, or drive recklessly.

People with Borderline Personality Disorder might also sometimes display reoccurring self-destructive behavior, gestures, or hazards, or self-mutilating actions. Completed self-destruction takes place in 8% -10% of such people, as well as self-mutilative acts (e.g., cutting or shedding) and suicide risks, as well as efforts, are extremely typical. Recurring suicidality is usually the reason that these people present for help. These suicidal acts are generally precipitated by hazards of splitting up or denial or by assumptions that they assume boosted duty. Self-mutilation may take place during dissociative experiences and frequently brings relief by declaring the capability to really feel or by expiating the individual's sense of profaning.

People with Borderline Personality Disorder may present affective instability that results from a marked reactivity of mood (e.g., intense anecdotal dysphoria, irritation, or stress and anxiety normally lasting a few hours and also just seldom greater than a few days). The standard dysphoric state of mind of those with Borderline Personality Disorder is typically interfered with by durations of temper, panic, or misery and is hardly ever eased by periods of health or satisfaction. These episodes might show the individual's severe sensitivity to social stress and anxieties.

People with Borderline Personality Disorder might be bothered by persistent sensations of vacuum. Individuals with Borderline Personality Conditions often reveal improper, extreme rage or have difficulty controlling their temper. The rage is usually elicited when a caregiver or enthusiast is seen as uncaring, withholding, passionless, or deserting.

During periods of extreme anxiety, transient paranoid ideation or dissociative signs (e.g., depersonalization) may happen, yet these are usually of not enough seriousness or duration to warrant an added medical diagnosis. The genuine or viewed return of the caretaker's nurturance may result in a remission of signs and symptoms.

IS THERE TREATMENT FOR BORDERLINE PERSONALITY DISORDER?

Simply as the signs differ from individual to person, so does the therapy. BPD is most definitely treatable, and at the really the very least, workable, once the issues are brought to daytime, and also the individual having a hard time recognizing what they are dealing with, as well as why they are acting that way.

HISTORY OF BPD

Borderline individuality has lots of signs and medical diagnostic criteria that "overlap" with various other mental illnesses. The conditions that share commonalities with BPD consist of depressive problems, bi-polar disorder, as well as schizophrenia, in addition to non-schizophrenic psychoses and anxiety problems. Borderline is typically misdiagnosed because several of the signs that develop the requirements to diagnose an individual as borderline are additionally signs and symptoms used to determine various other ailments. As a matter of fact, it utilized to be called a "wastebasket" medical diagnosis. Psychology made use of to watch borderline as the category psychoanalysts would put clients in when they really did not satisfy the certain criteria for any other diagnoses, which utilized to be taken into consideration a lot more "diagnostically precise and valid" than BPD. Borderline personality disorder has made substantial strides in the mental field earning respect, legitimacy, as well as research on treatment alternatives, but regrettably, some experts still see it as the diagnostic "wastebasket.".

The presence of borderline personality disorder first came to the attention of psychotherapists in the very early 1900s. Adolph Stern was the initial psychoanalyst to identify it. It began with him identifying a team of clients who had no feedback on timeless psychoanalytical treatment around 1938. Adolph Stern described these people and also their manifesting signs and symptoms as getting on the line between neurosis and also psychosis, and as a result, classified them "the borderline team." He was the first to coin the term "borderline." Although Adolph Stern brought the idea of BPD to the mental area, it would be years before the mental disorder would certainly be approved as a true emotional term. Lots of experts reviewed and defined the phenomena of BPD before it was officially sworn in into the Diagnostic and also Statistical Handbook III, though. Gregory Zilboorg, a psychoanalyst and also medical historian, defined the disorder as a much more moderate version of schizophrenia in 1941. Helene Deutsch, the first psychoanalyst to focus on ladies, gone over people who depended on others' characters in her research in the 1940s also. This reliance, which is now part of the standards for the diagnosis of BPD, was defined as an "as-if personality" by Deutsch. In 1967, Otto Kernberg, who is currently the

Director of the Individuality Disorders Institute at the New York-Presbyterian Hospital, Westchester Division, in addition to a Teacher of Psychiatry at the Weill Cornell Medication, built on Adolph Stern's ideas regarding BPD. Kernberg specifically defined the limits between neurosis as well as psychosis. Like Stern, he put borderline personality disorder in the middle.

Roy Grinker was the first to officially do research on borderline personality disorder. In 1968, he published The Borderline Syndrome, a publication that contained "the first reported results of a lengthy study program on hospitalized borderline individuals whose ego-functions were studied via multiple monitorings on their daily habits." Even with this publication, though, BPD was not officially identified as a medical diagnosis in the Diagnostic and Statistical Handbook.

John G. Gunderson was a psychoanalyst that also published research to assist detect borderline. Presently the Supervisor of McLean Healthcare facility's Borderline Center, as well as a professor at Harvard, Gunderson, is an expert that helped confirm borderline personality disorder as an internationally recognized illness as opposed to a psychoanalytic construct. Known as the "dad" of BPD, Gunderson's work, as well as a research study in 1975, helped borderline be consisted of in the DSM-III in 1980.

Research study started on exactly how to treat it as soon as BPD was officially a confirmed condition. As had actually been recognized from the get-go, borderline individuals did not respond to classical psychoanalytic therapy, like psychiatric therapy and drug. In 1993, Marsha Linehan established the concept of dialectical behavior therapy(DBT). She introduced this as an efficient treatment for borderline patients. DBT is based on the idea that the emotion dysregulation in borderline individuals is the core one, as well as drives all various other dysregulations they experience. It concentrates on recognizing assuming disorders, and also consequently giving borderline people the tools to acknowledge and also attempt to transform the filters that impact their actions as well as reactions. Dialectical behavior therapy is still considered one of the most effective treatments for borderline personality disorder.

The validity, as well as recognition of BPD, has actually remained to enhance throughout the years. When the DSM-

IV was published in 1994, it had extra certain symptoms of borderline required for an exact medical diagnosis. Now May is also known as the National Borderline Personality Disorder Recognition Month and has been since 2008. Research, as well as research studies concerning BPD, proceed today, with lots of practicing experts in the field as well as many people studying to become like them.

SIGNS AND SYMPTOMS

Borderline personality disorder (BPD) manifests in many different ways, but for the purposes of diagnosis, mental health professionals group the symptoms into nine major categories. In order to be diagnosed with BPD, you must show signs of at least five of these symptoms. Furthermore, the symptoms must be long-standing (usually beginning in adolescence) and impact many areas of your life.

9 Symptoms of BCD

1. People with BPD are typically frightened of being deserted or left alone. Even something as harmless as a loved one arriving house late from a job or going away for the weekend may cause intense fear. You might plead, cling, begin battles, track your liked one's emotions, or also literally obstruct the individual from leaving.

2. People with BPD have a tendency to have connections that are temporary, as well as intense. You may drop in love promptly, thinking that each new individual is the one that will certainly make

you really feel entire, only to be rapidly disappointed.

3. Uncertain or changing self-image. Your feeling of self is commonly unstable when you have BPD. In some cases, you may really feel great regarding your own; however, various other times you despise on your own or perhaps watch yourself as evil. You most likely do not have a clear idea of who you are or what you want in life. Consequently, you might regularly transform jobs, pals, lovers, religious beliefs, values, objectives, or even sexual identification.

4. If you have BPD, you might engage in unsafe, sensation-seeking behaviors, especially when you're upset. These risky actions may help you feel better in the minute; however they hurt you and those around you over the long-term.

5. Suicidal behavior and intentional self-harm are typical in individuals with BPD. Suicidal actions consist of believing regarding self-destruction, making suicidal gestures or risks, or actually carrying out a self-destruction attempt.

6. Extreme psychological swings. Unstable emotions and also moods prevail with BPD. One minute, you may rejoice, as well as the next, negative. Little things that individuals sweep aside can send you right into a psychological tailspin. These mood swings are intense, but they often tend to pass fairly rapidly (unlike the emotional swings of anxiety or bipolar illness), usually lasting simply a few minutes or hrs.

7. Persistent feelings of vacuum. People with BPD typically talk about feeling vacant, as if there's a hole or space inside them. At the severe, you may really feel as if you're "nothing" or "no one." This sensation is unpleasant, so you may attempt to fill the void with things like medicines, food, or sex. Absolutely nothing feels truly pleasing.

8. If you have BPD, you might struggle with extreme temper and a brief temper. It's crucial to keep in mind that this anger isn't constantly directed in an outward direction.

9. Feeling dubious or out of touch with reality. Individuals with BPD typically deal with paranoia or questionable thoughts concerning others'

motives. When under anxiety, you may also lose touch with reality-- an experience referred to as dissociation. You might feel foggy, spaced out, or as if you're outside your own body.

These signs and symptoms can create substantial psychological pain and also discomfort, as well as they can have substantial real-world consequences (self-destruction prices among BPD victims are an amazing 10 percent).

If their problem remains undiagnosed or is left neglected, borderline character disorder patients might live in a state of perpetual mayhem or change. They may be exceptionally delicate to objection, to the point where even casual statements might speed up an emotional situation.

As a result of their emotional instability, BPD sufferers might struggle to locate or hold work, frequently change their life strategies or belief systems, often jump in and out of friendships or charming connections, get mixed up with cults, or end up being consumed with self-help gurus. They may be drawn to people that actually do abuse and misuse them, including new layers of trauma onto a currently tight spot. They might discover happiness elusive, and their capacity to be successful can be significantly jeopardized.

BPD in People

Despite the most up to date findings that recommend women, as well as males, deal with borderline personality disorder similarly, ladies are still being detected even more frequently. When men with BPD signs and symptoms request for help (which doesn't always occur), they often tend to be misdiagnosed with various other problems, such as bipolar illness, ADHD, post-traumatic stress disorder (PTSD), intermittent explosive disorder, or clinical depression.

Some mental health professionals might have an unconscious bias that assumes BPD is far more common in ladies, which might disrupt their capability to find BPD in males even when it exists. Since females are treated more regularly, their signs have actually obtained a default condition as the "main" face of borderline personality problem, making it hard for psychiatrists as well as psychotherapists to acknowledge BPD signs in males that do not fairly fit their assumptions.

The total symptomatic profile for a borderline personality disorder is mainly the very same for women as well as males. There are some distinctions in the method the signs of BPD show up in the 2 genders.

In general, guys with BPD are:

- Extremely conscious objection, and hostile in response to perceived disrespects or put-downs
- Extremely controlling in connections
- Possessive and also extremely jealous
- Quick to become disillusioned with others, and freely meaningful of their ridicule
- Subject to mood changes that occur in a split second
- Prone as well as exceedingly short-tempered to episodes of eruptive temper
- Likely to compensate for sensations of inadequacy via risky, dangerous habits

As this list reveals, BPD in males usually has an assertive or aggressive side, which is not viewed as frequently with BPD in women.

This can bring about unsympathetic as well as undesirable behavior that alienates others and also leads them to react in anger. Rather than using help or inspiration, relative and also friends might abandon or distance themselves from men with BPD, and also without loved ones motivating them to look for the assistance they might never identify the nature and also the depth of their problem.

Co-occurring problems prevail among BPD patients, but ladies with BPD are most likely to have numerous disorders than guys. In virtually every category of co-occurring disease, ladies have greater prices of medical diagnosis. There are two significant exemptions to this pattern.

Initially, men with BPD are most likely to create a material use disorder than women with BPD (58 percent versus 44 percent past-year incidence in one study). Second, they are far more likely to be detected with an antisocial personality disorder, which is far from unexpected given the hostility as well as aggression that so often accompanies BPD in males.

Alcohol and also drug abuse are an acquainted coping mechanism for people with psychological health disorders, as well as men with borderline personality disorder have a lifetime danger for chemical abuse of above 80 percent. Due to their drug abuse issues, males with BPD often choose alcohol as well as medicine rehab over other types of treatment, inaccurately presuming all of their troubles are triggered by drugs and alcohol.

BPD in Adolescents and Children

Teenagers have a tendency to experience the exact same signs and symptoms as grownups dealing with borderline personality disorders.

Nevertheless, they may not develop sufficient of those signs to get a BPD diagnosis (5 of the 9 main signs must exist in some type for a medical diagnosis to be made). What many teenagers (and also youngsters) experience is BPD in development, where a structure is established for future experiences with a full-on variation of the problem.

Kids can also show the qualities of borderline personality disorder. Kids exhibiting BPD indicators tend to manifest what is typically categorized as childish behaviors, just in an extra exaggerated kind.

In comparison to other children, they are much more:

- Demanding of time and attention

- Prone to outbursts and fits of craze

- Conveniently distressed

- Agitated as well as undistinct

- Sensitive to objection

- Likely to suffer splitting up stress and anxiety

- Subject to physical signs and symptoms of anxiety (stomach pains, migraines, consuming or ingesting troubles, etc.).

It is simple to see why such signs of BPD could be forgotten or disregarded as "kids being youngsters." Diagnosing borderline personality disorder in kids is a challenging procedure, and any individual with a child experiencing signs constant with the problem needs to speak with a kid psychoanalyst for examination and also recommendations.

CAUSES AND RISK FACTORS

If you or a liked one has a borderline personality disorder (BPD), you may be wondering what created it or if you are to blame. The development of this condition is intricate, and also there is likely a range of borderline personality disorder causes, and also, you must rest assured that no person or thing is at fault.

Many specialists think that BPD establishes as a result of organic, genetic, and also ecological elements. Nevertheless, it is important to remember that the exact sources of BPD are not known yet. Right now, these are concepts that have some assistance in assistance but are by no means conclusive. More research study is needed to identify exactly how and why the elements gone over below relate to BPD.

Prospective Environmental Borderline Personality Disorder Creates

There is solid proof to support a link between traumatic youth experiences, specifically including caregivers, and

BPD. The types of experiences that may be associated with BPD consist of:

- Physical as well as sex-related abuse
- Early splitting up from caregivers
- Physical or emotional disregard
- Adult ignorance

It is assumed that communication between biological elements (reviewed below) as well as a revoking childhood years setting may work together in predisposing an individual to establish BPD. An emotionally revoking environment is one in which a kid's emotional needs are not fulfilled.

A revoking setting is not always apparent to those that have actually experienced it or to others around them. These agonizing experiences can be concealed as well as also camouflaged as appreciation.

Potential Genetic and Biological Borderline Personality Disorder Causes

While early studies showed that BPD does have a tendency to run in the family members, for some time, it was not known whether this was as a result of environmental impacts or because of genetics. There is currently some proof that in addition to the environment, genetic elements play a substantial duty.

Particularly, research studies have actually shown that a variant in genetics that controls the method the mind uses serotonin (a natural chemical in the brain) may be connected to BPD. It appears that individuals who have this particular variant of the serotonin gene may be more likely to establish BPD if they also experience challenging childhood years occasions (for example, separation from helpful caretakers).

One research study located that monkeys with the serotonin gene variation developed signs and symptoms that looked similar to BPD, but just when they were drawn from their mothers and raised in much less nurturing settings. Monkeys with the gene variant who were increased by supporting moms were a lot less likely to create BPD-like symptoms.

As an example, individuals with BPD have much more activation of the limbic system, an area of the brain that manages aggressiveness, fear, and also anger, than people without BPD. This might be connected to the emotional instability symptoms of BPD. Newer research studies are additionally searchings for related to the hormone oxytocin as well as the advancement of BPD.

Bottom Line on the Causes of Borderline Personality Disorder

There is much to be learned about the sources of BPD, and also it's most likely that it is a mix of variables as opposed to any kind of one certain searching for which can bring about the condition. The study is in development and hopefully we will discover more in the coming years.

Recognizing the reasons may assist in preventing the beginning of the disorder, specifically in those that have a genetic or biological tendency to the condition. As it is, a revoking setting is dangerous to a kid, whether it elevates the probability of BPD in the future, as well as it is critical for therapists to be sharp for this setting in kids.

Because an invalidating setting can be hidden, with many remarks seeming comments of appreciation on the surface, feelings can quickly be mistaken as an oversensitivity for the kid rather than a lack of sensitivity on the part of the parent. It is essential for grownups who experienced emotional invalidation as a child to learn to recognize the difference between verifying and also invalidating comments from others to safeguard themselves from further hurt.

RISK FACTORS

Some elements connected to individuality advancement can boost the risk of developing a borderline personality disorder. These consist of:

- Genetic proneness. You might go to a greater threat if a close loved one-- your mother, sister, papa or brother-- has the very same or a comparable disorder.
- Stressful childhood.Numerous individuals with the problem report being sexually or physically overused or disregarded throughout the childhood years. Some individuals had actually shed or were divided from mom and dad or close caregiver when they were young or had moms and dads or

caretakers with material misuse or other mental health and wellness problems.

COMPLICATIONS

Borderline personality disorder can harm many areas of your life. It can adversely affect intimate partnerships, tasks, college, social tasks, and also self-image, leading to:

- Repeated task changes or losses
- Not completing an education and learning
- Multiple legal problems, such as prison time
- Conflict-filled relationships, marital stress and anxiety or separation
- Self-injury, such as reducing or shedding, and also constant hospital stays
- Participation in violent connections
- Unplanned maternities, sexually transferred infections, car accidents and also physical battles due to risky and also impulsive actions
- Attempted or finished suicide

Additionally, you may have other psychological health conditions, such as:

- Anxiety.

- Alcohol or other chemical misuses.

- Anxiousness problems.

- Eating disorders.

- Bipolar disorder.

- Post-traumatic stress disorder (PTSD).

- Attention-deficit/hyperactivity disorder (ADHD).

- Various other personality disorders.

Facts About BPD

Borderline personality disorder (BPD) is a commonly exceptionally misinterpreted mental health and wellness condition generally conflated with bipolar disorder. In truth, it's an entirely various mental illness. Take a few minutes to review the truths listed below and also much better understand borderline personality disorder, in addition to individuals that live with it.

1. Borderline personality disorder often causes signs and symptoms like extreme mood shifts and unpredictability in exactly how an individual watches themselves and others.

Individuals with BPD often tend to have problem regulating emotions, an unsteady sense of self, as well as a pattern of intense, unsteady connections. At its core, BPD affects exactly how a person feels as well as believes regarding themselves and also others sufficient to negatively impact their everyday life.

The Diagnostic as well as Statistical Guidebook, which mental health and wellness specialists utilize to detect mental illnesses, needs that a person displays at the very least 5 of the complying with signs in order to get a BPD diagnosis:

- Panicked efforts to stay clear of abandonment (whether genuine or fictional).
- A pattern of unstable and also intense connections that vacillate between fondness as well as love (idealization) to do not like or temper (decline).
- A poor or unpredictable feeling of self.
- Spontaneous as well as dangerous habits in a minimum of 2 possibly dangerous locations, like spending a great deal of cash or having harmful sex-related encounters.
- Self-harm or suicidal behavior/threats.
- Extreme mood moves that generally last a couple of hours.
- Really feeling vacant.
- Temper control issues.
- Really feeling removed from oneself or truth.

It's possible to experience a mix of these signs and symptoms and not have a borderline personality disorder. The indications require to be phenomenal as well as consistent in order to meet the standards for this condition.

Or, as an additional example, many individuals without BPD have a fear of individuals they like or love leaving them. But individuals with BPD often experience this so extremely that they have a difficult time relying on others and also will preemptively reduce people out of their lives.

2. BPD is thought to impact about 1 percent of individuals in the United States.

The 2007 National Comorbidity Survey Duplication published in Biological Psychiatry offers an estimate of the number of individuals have actually BPD. The nationally representative research study checked out 5,692 people, discovering that while the frequency of any personality disorder was around 9 percent, only 1.4 percent of respondents met the analysis requirements for BPD in particular.

3. Individuals with BPD often have other psychological health and wellness conditions.

According to The National Comorbidity Study Duplication, 84.5 percent of participants with BPD had a co-occurring mental wellness problem.

The nature of these comorbidities differs from person to person and can make acknowledging BPD hard. Extreme episodes of clinical depression can be a symptom of BPD; however they can also be the outcome of a problem like the major depressive problem or bipolar disorder.

The partnership between BPD and also other problems is not completely recognized. When it comes to something like a substance usage disorder, it may be an unfavorable coping system to take care of the unpleasant signs of BPD. The feelings of desertion as well as alienation (from oneself and others), along with a lack of steady and close relationships, might speed up anxiety.

4. Borderline personality disorder as well as bipolar disorder are not the exact same point.

They do share some significant similarities, specifically that bipolar disorder likewise triggers severe changes in the state of mind and also behavior. Those shifts are mainly between manic as well as depressive episodes (having energy as well as abnormally raised state of mind) or hypomanic episodes, which also entail abnormally high energy and task degrees however, to a lesser extent. The worry of abandonment as well as unsteady personal relationships that are usually inherent to BPD isn't in the analysis standards for bipolar problems.

5. People with BPD are at a raised danger for self-harm and also self-destruction as a result of a mix of intense emotions and impulsivity.

Together with self-harm, suicidal ideation, as well as habits and, are substantially a lot more common amongst people with BPD. The usually accepted number cited by the American Psychiatric Organization approximates that 8 to 10 percent of individuals with BPD will certainly pass away by suicide, which is tragically high. Keeping that claimed, it is necessary to remember that because the price of suicide efforts in this community is so elevated (some resources claim as high as 60 to 70 percent), the number of completed suicides is thankfully less than it could be.

Individuals with BPD may resort to self-harm due to the fact that it seems like immediate alleviation for enhanced feelings. Likewise, someone may attempt suicide as spontaneous ways of coping with the deep psychological suffering BPD can trigger.

6. There is no single root cause of BPD, yet professionals think there are several essential danger aspects entailed.

According to a research study recommends that a mix of hereditary, neurological, and also environmental variables raises a person's likelihood of having BPD.

If a relative has BPD, you're more probable to also have it, yet there is no well-known genetics connected to the condition. It also appears as though the minds of individuals with BPD have structural as well as practical changes in locations related to points like psychological regulation, yet it's unclear if those changes are a reason or outcome of the problem. As well as when it concerns ecological aspects, many people with BPD record circumstances of childhood trauma, consisting of abuse, desertion, as well as unsteady connections with their moms and dads.

7. Some experts advocate for detecting BPD in teenagers while others favor waiting till the adult years.

There has been basic hesitation in identifying personality disorders in those under 18., in some cases, what seems like BPD can merely be part of a youngster or young adult's psychological growth.

With that said said, medical professionals, are finding that BPD can be detected in teenagers and youngsters. Feasible indicators are similar to those in adults as well as consist of impulsive risk-taking, regular angry outbursts, continual social issues, significantly low self-esteem, and recurring self-injury or self-destruction attempts.

The earlier we interfere, the more likely we are to aid.

8. The first-line therapy for BPD is treatment.

The goal is to aid our clients develop psychological guideline muscles, in a manner of speaking, to make sure that they will be able to stand up to the influence of those psychological [waves] We can not remove their emotional sensitivity, however, we can give them abilities to [better] reply to the emotional reaction. One technique for this is dialectical behavior therapy(DBT), which combines approval and mindfulness of one's emotional state with coping skills for these feelings. Cognitive behavior therapy(CBT), which can assist individuals with BPD, determine as well as manage their habits and feelings, is another usual alternative.

9. It can be hard for a person with BPD to trust their therapist, however, that bond is typically foundational to recuperation.

This is why specialists dealing with BPD typically stress approval and also recognition. (There is a crucial difference in between approving a statement or habits--" I recognize why you did that"-- and also excusing it--" Good job, maintain doing that.").

Individually model, team sessions led by a therapist can also aid individuals with BPD discover exactly how to finest communicate with and also express themselves to various other individuals.

There are none medications particularly advised to treat BPD.

There merely aren't yet clear adequate benefits to using medications as the main therapy for BPD.

A psychoanalyst may recommend the drug to address specific signs and symptoms that some individuals experience, such as state of mind stabilizers for psychological instability. Furthermore, somebody with BPD who likewise has a scientifically diagnosed co-occurring disorder, such as PTSD, anxiety, or anxiety, might take drugs to deal with those problems.

BPD is often stigmatized, even among healthcare providers.

A 2013 testimonial of readily available literary works released in Developments in Scientific Neuroscience discovered that some psychological health service providers hold harmful as well as false sights on BPD. Laypeople can think of these myths, also.

Among one of the most pervasive misperceptions among non-professionals and specialists alike is that people with

BPD are deliberately, maliciously attempting to manipulate those around them with their screens of extreme emotion or self-harm. This is false. These signs are coming from mental disease, not a person deciding their very own choice that they 'd like to adjust to other individuals.

People with BPD can be empathetic as well as lovely individuals.

Extreme emotional level of sensitivity offers with major difficulties, but there are additional advantages. In her experience, people with BPD are often able to recognize the sensations of other people better. She also believes that lots of people with BPD are uncommonly creative due to the fact that they have a much deeper and broader experience of human feeling where to draw.

This belongs to the reason that people with BPD are her preferred populace to treat. "They are really fun, innovative, thoughtful, beautiful people.

Diagnosis and Treatment

Diagnosis: This focuses on two potential kinds of viewers in mind psychological health and wellness customers (i.e., clients) and also mental wellness companies. I really hope to illustrate that even with a medical diagnosis that some providers may shy away from going over with their patients, there is, at the very least one means to make a respectful technique.

Throughout several treatment setups, I have frequently obtained brand-new client references whose history, as well as scientific presentation, fits very well with the diagnosis of BPD. As well as what I find is that in the substantial bulk of cases, individuals have no suggestion that borderline individuality disorder is their charted medical diagnosis.

My theory is that also amongst extremely enlightened mental health and wellness companies; borderline personality disorder is a medical diagnosis that motivates a fear/avoidance response. I can think of no other apparent reason these patients so usually have no idea what ails them in spite of years of treatment (commonly with multiple suppliers, as this is in some cases part of the professional photo).

Clinically depressed people understand what their medical diagnosis is. Nervous people recognize what their medical diagnosis is. Clients with psychotic problems are usually informed concerning their condition. Substance reliance issues are reviewed freely, and also relapses are generally charted. Yet borderline patients are often left at night.

As a theme, individuals with borderline personality disorder have characteristic difficulties with attachments to others, usually due to vulnerabilities in their very early lives. Individuals with BPD have severe difficulty controlling their own feelings, maintaining healthy close relationships, and also holding onto a strong sense of their very own identifications. This is not the fault of these patients. Many borderline people I see are experiencing really minimal understanding right into their problem. Many do absent like Angelina Jolie in the flick "Lady, Interrupted"-- intriguing, manipulative people to be prevented in any way prices.

Occasionally, they are combat-trained men with significant muscular tissues, who are enduring.

I figure that if we as carriers are to have a possibility to develop a better add-on to these patients, it is crucial to begin by talking fact, in a respectful way. I have actually been refining my strategy to this discussion for some years, and also I'm sure it's not excellent; however it has never ever resulted in any kind of individual lashing out at me or promptly dropping out of treatment.

I ask the individual if he or she has ever before heard of BPD. It is essential to discover out what the person knows as well as whether he or she comes in with prospective unwarranted negative impressions of what BPD is.

Personality disorders, consisting of borderline personality disorder, are identified based on a:

An in-depth interview with your doctor or psychological wellness carrier

An emotional examination that might include completing questionnaires

Case history as well as test

The conversation of your symptoms and signs

A medical diagnosis of borderline personality disorder is normally made in grownups, not in young adults or kids. That's since what seems symptoms and signs of borderline personality disorder may go away as kids grow older and become elder.

TREATMENT

A borderline personality disorder is mainly treated using psychotherapy, but medication may be added. Your doctor also may recommend hospitalization if your safety is at risk.

Treatment can help you learn skills to manage and cope with your condition. It's also necessary to get treated for any other mental health disorders that often occur along with borderline personality disorder, such as depression or substance misuse. With treatment, you can feel better about yourself and live a more stable, rewarding life.

Psychotherapy

A borderline personality disorder is primarily dealt with by making use of psychotherapy, however, drug might be added. Your medical professional also may suggest a hospital stay if your security is at threat.

Treatment can assist you to discover the abilities to handle and cope with your condition. It's additionally needed to get treated for any other mental health and wellness problems that typically happen in addition to borderline personality disorder, such as anxiety or substance misuse. With therapy, you can feel far better regarding yourself and live an extra steady, fulfilling life.

Psychotherapy

Psychotherapy, also called talk treatment, is a basic therapy method for borderline personality disorder. Your therapist might adjust the sort of therapy to the finest meet your requirements. The objectives of psychotherapy are to assist you:

- Concentrate on your present capacity to work
- Find out to manage feelings that really feel awkward
- Decrease your impulsiveness by aiding you to observe sensations as opposed to acting upon them
- Deal with boosting connections by recognizing your sensations and also those of others
- Find out about borderline personality disorder

Types of psychotherapy that have been discovered to be effective include:

- Dialectical behavior therapy (DBT). DBT includes team and specific treatment designed particularly to treat borderline personality disorder. DBT uses a skills-based strategy to instruct you on how to handle your feelings, endure distress and also enhance relationships.

- Schema-focused therapy. Therapy concentrates on assisting you in obtaining your demands satisfied in a healthy and balanced fashion to promote positive life patterns.

- Mentalization-based treatment (MBT). MBT is a sort of talk treatment that assists you in determining your own ideas and also feelings at any kind of given minute and create an alternate perspective on the circumstance. MBT stresses assuming before responding.

- Systems training for emotional predictability as well as for analytic (STEPPS). STEPPS is a 20-week treatment that entails working in groups that incorporate your family members, caretakers, friends or loved ones right into therapy. STEPPS is utilized along with other sorts of psychotherapy.

- Transference-focused psychotherapy (TFP). Called psychodynamic psychiatric therapy, TFP aims to assist you in understanding your emotions and also social difficulties via the developing partnership in between you and your specialist. You then use these understandings to continuous scenarios.

- Good psychiatric monitoring. It may incorporate drugs, groups, family members education and learning and individual therapy.

Medications

Although no drugs have been accepted by the Fda specifically for the therapy of borderline personality disorder, certain drugs may help with signs and symptoms or co-occurring issues such as depression, stress, and anxiety, aggressiveness, or impulsiveness. Medicines might include antidepressants, antipsychotics or mood-stabilizing medications.

Speak with your medical professional regarding the benefits and side effects of medications.

Hospitalization

Sometimes, you may need more-intense treatment in a psychiatric hospital or facility. A hospital stay might also keep you safe from self-injury or address suicidal thoughts or actions.

Healing takes some time

Learning to manage your ideas, habits, as well as emotions, takes time. Most individuals improve substantially, yet you might always fight with some symptoms of borderline personality disorder. You may experience times when your signs are much better or worse. But treatment can enhance your capability to work and also help you really feel much better about yourself.

When you consult a psychological health carrier who has experience treating borderline character problem, you have the finest chance for success.

TYPES OF PSYCHOTHERAPY

Borderline personality disorder (BPD) is a difficulty to treat not only because it is complicated and stigmatized, but also because its signs show embedded patterns of believing and behavior. Although it is heterogeneous in nature, causing various collections of signs in different individuals, the disorder has 3 major scientific components: a vulnerable feeling of self that harms connections with other people, impulsiveness, and also psychological volatility. Several patients with BPD also have various other psychological health issues, such as a mood disorder or post-traumatic stress disorder.

Medications might be moderately handy at reducing specific signs and symptoms, such as clinical depression or stress and anxiety; however they do not resolve core characteristics as well as behaviors. Psychiatric therapy continues to be the pillar of therapy for clients with BPD, although there is no "one-size-fits-all" therapy.

Dialectical behavior therapy is possibly the most common psychiatric therapy made use of for BPD, but other choices have arisen. A testimonial of 4 psychiatric therapies concluded that all were equally effective general, but that each had particular benefits. Because of this, individuals and also medical professionals can decide on an individual basis which treatment is most ideal.

The effect of BPD extends well past the specific client, triggering suffering in family members also. Enjoyed ones, like therapists, might battle with how to respond constructively to an individual's unstable moods and also demands. Therefore, a relative might likewise gain from psychiatric therapy.

COGNITIVE BEHAVIORAL THERAPY (CBT).

Cognitive behavior therapy(CBT) is a kind of psychotherapeutic treatment that assists individuals to comprehend the thoughts and also sensations that affect behaviors. CBT is generally utilized to treat a wide range of problems, including anxieties, dependencies, depression, and also anxiety.

Cognitive behavior therapy is generally short-term as well as focused on helping clients take care of a very specific problem. Throughout the program of treatment, individuals discover just how to identify and change disturbing or harmful idea patterns that have an unfavorable impact on actions and also emotions.

Cognitive Behavioral Therapy Basics.

The underlying concept behind CBT is that our ideas and feelings play a fundamental function in our habits. A person that spends a great deal of time thinking concerning plane crashes, path crashes, and also various other air catastrophes may discover themselves preventing air traveling.

The objective of cognitive behavior therapy is to show clients that while they can not manage every element of the world around them, they can take control of how they deal as well as translate with points in their setting.

Cognitive behavior therapy has actually come to be progressively popular in the last few years with both psychological health and wellness consumers and therapy specialists. It is frequently a lot more economical than some other types of treatment because CBT is generally a short-term therapy alternative. CBT is also empirically sustained and also has actually been shown to properly assist people in getting over a wide variety of maladaptive habits.

The Background of Cognitive Behavioral Therapy.

Cognitive behavior therapy was invented by a psychiatrist, Aaron Beck, in the 1960s. He was doing psychoanalysis at the time as well as observed that during his logical sessions, his patients had a tendency to have an internal discussion taking place in their minds-- practically as if they were talking to themselves. They would only report a portion of this kind of thinking to him.

In a therapy session, the customer might be thinking to herself: "He (the specialist) hasn't claimed much today. These thoughts might make the client really feel maybe annoyed or slightly distressed.

He developed the term automatic ideas to explain emotion-filled ideas that could stand out up in mind. Beck found that people weren't always totally mindful of such ideas, but might find out to determine and report them.

Because of the importance, it positions on reasoning, Beck called it cognitive treatment. It's now known as cognitive-behavioral therapy (CBT) due to the fact that the treatment uses behavior techniques also. The equilibrium between the cognitive and also the behavioral components differs amongst the various treatments of this kind. However all come under the umbrella term cognitive behavior therapy. CBT has actually given that undertaken effective clinical trials in many locations by various teams and has been applied to a wide array of troubles.

The Importance of Negative Ideas.

CBT is based on a design or concept that it's not occasioned themselves that dismayed us, but the significances we provide. If our ideas are as well adverse, it can block us seeing points or doing things that do not fit-- that disconfirm-- what we believe is true. Simply put, we continue to hold on to the same old thoughts and stop working to find out anything brand-new.

A depressed lady may assume, "I can not face going right into work today: I can't do it. As a result of having these thoughts-- as well as of believing them-- she may well ring in unwell. Believing, feeling as well as acting like this may begin a descending spiral.

Where Do These Negative Thoughts Come From?

Beck suggested that these assuming patterns are set up in childhood years, and become automated as well as reasonably fixed. A child who really did not get much open love from their parents but was applauded for an institution's job may come to assume, "I have to do well all the time.

However, if something occurs that's beyond their control and they experience failure, then the useless thought pattern might be triggered. The individual may after that, start to have automated thoughts like, "I've totally failed. No person will like me. I can not encounter them."

Cognitive-behavioral therapy acts to aid the person to understand that this is what's going on. In the light of an extra practical point of view, she might be able to take the chance of examining out what other individuals think, by revealing something of her problems to close friends.

Clearly, negative things can as well as do take place. But when we remain in a disrupted state of mind, we might be basing our forecasts and analyses on a prejudiced view of the situation, making the problem that we deal with appear much even worse. CBT assists people to deal with these misconceptions.

Sorts Of Cognitive Behavior Therapy

According to the British Association of Behavioural and also Cognitive Psychotherapies, "Cognitive as well as behavior psychotherapies are a range of therapies based on principles and concepts originated from mental designs of human emotion and actions. They include a large range of therapy methods for emotional disorders, along with a continuum from organized private psychiatric therapy to self-help product."

There are a variety of particular kinds of restorative approaches that entail CBT that is on a regular basis utilized by psychological health and wellness professionals. Examples of these include:

Sensible Stirring Behavior Therapy (REBT): This kind of CBT is centered on identifying and altering illogical ideas. The process of REBT includes recognizing the underlying irrational ideas, proactively challenging these beliefs, and also lastly, learning to recognize and change these believed patterns.

Cognitive Therapy: This type of therapy is fixated identifying as well as altering inaccurate or distorted reasoning patterns, psychological responses, and also habits.

Multimodal Therapy: This kind of CBT recommends that psychological issues should be dealt with by addressing 7 different but interconnected techniques, which are actions, affect, feeling, imagery, cognition, drug/biological considerations and interpersonal factors.

Dialectical Behavior Modification: This kind of cognitive-behavioral therapy addresses believing patterns and behaviors as well as incorporates approaches such as psychological law as well as mindfulness.

While each sort of cognitive-behavioral therapy offers its very own one-of-a-kind technique, each fixates resolving the underlying idea patterns that contribute to emotional distress.

The Components of Cognitive Behavior Therapy

Individuals often experience ideas or sensations that strengthen or intensify malfunctioning beliefs. Such beliefs can cause troublesome habits that can impact countless life areas, including family, romantic relationships, work, and academics.

A person experiencing low self-worth might experience unfavorable thoughts regarding his or her very own capabilities or look. As a result of these negative attitude patterns, the individual may start staying clear of social circumstances or pass up opportunities for innovation at work or at the institution.

In order to fight these destructive ideas and also actions, a cognitive-behavioral specialist begins by helping the client to recognize the problematic beliefs. This stage, called useful evaluation, is essential for learning how scenarios, feelings, as well as ideas can add to maladaptive actions. The procedure can be difficult, especially for people that struggle with self-contemplation, yet it can inevitably bring about self-discovery as well as insights that are a vital part of the treatment procedure.

The 2nd part of cognitive behavior therapy focuses on the actual actions that are contributing to the trouble. The client begins to discover as well as exercise brand-new abilities that can then be put in to utilize in real-world situations. For example, a person struggling with medicine addiction may start exercising new coping skills and practicing methods to deal with or avoid social scenarios that might possibly trigger a regression.

CBT is a progressive procedure that helps a person takes incremental steps towards a behavior therapy. A person struggling with social anxiety may begin by just imagining himself in an anxiety-provoking social circumstance.

Next, the customer could begin exercising conversations with friends, family members, as well as acquaintances. By considerably working toward a larger objective, the process seems much less daunting and also the objectives simpler to accomplish.

The Process of Cognitive Behavior therapy.

Throughout the procedure of CBT, the specialist tends to take a very energetic role.

CBT is highly ambitious and focused, and the customer and also specialists work together as collaborators towards the equally established goals.

The specialist will generally clarify the process thoroughly, and the client will commonly be provided with research to complete between sessions.

Cognitive-behavior therapy can be efficiently made use of as a temporary treatment centered on assisting the client deal with really details trouble.

Uses of Cognitive Behavior Therapy.

Cognitive behavior therapy has actually been used to treat people suffering from a variety of conditions, consisting of:

- Anxiousness.
- Phobias.
- Anxiety.
- Dependencies.
- Eating disorders.
- Panic attacks.
- Anger.

CBT is one of the most researched kinds of treatment, partially since therapy is focused on very certain objectives and also results can be gauged relatively easily.

Contrasted to psychoanalytic types of psychiatric therapy which encourage a more flexible self-exploration, cognitive behavior therapy is often best-suited for customers who are much more comfy with an organized and focused method in which the specialist frequently takes an instructional function. However, for CBT to be reliable, the private should be ready and also ready to hang out and effort is assessing his or her thoughts and also sensations. Such self-analysis as well as homework can be tough, however it is a terrific method to get more information regarding exactly how internal states impact outward behavior.

Cognitive behavior therapy is also well-suited for individuals trying to find a short-term treatment choice for sure types of psychological distress that does not necessarily involve psychotropic drugs. One of the greatest benefits of cognitive-behavior therapy is that it helps customers establish dealing skills that can be helpful both currently and in the future.

What did you think when you started to really feel distressed prior to your test? What do you do when you start to feel upset?

What to expect in therapy

While a CBT-oriented specialist may ask you regarding your childhood and also past to better recognize the setting you grew up in such as, whether there might be a family background of psychological health and wellness trouble the emphasis in sessions is on comprehending what is taking place inside you when psychological issues arise as well as helping you do the exact same. What topics does your brain focus on? Just how do you talk to yourself when you're really feeling depressed as well as really feel that you can't obtain out of bed?

Recognition is the front door to alter, and also by being aware of your reactions. You currently can start to change them-- both the ideas as well as the habits. That being claimed, the adjustment is not immediate: If you do change your actions and/or thoughts, you ought to anticipate that your sensations will certainly remain the same for some time-- that you will certainly feel guilty if you didn't volunteer for that committee at church even though you stated to on your own that you truly don't have the moment; that you will really feel distressed that you really did not that you didn't get all the laundry done on the weekend break like you usually do; that if you require on your own out of bed, you will likely still really feel depressed.

This is due to the fact that feelings drag ideas and behaviors. You require to duplicate developing these new thoughts and habits sometimes prior to you develop new circuits in your brain. You also require to intentionally pat yourself on the back, even with just how you really feel, for damaging old ideas as well as behavior patterns.

Just how to use this by yourself

While a CBT-oriented specialist can aid you to boost your recognition and discover these abilities, as well as aid you to remain accountable for using them, you can do this by yourself. There are lots of workbooks that you can make use of to aid you to establish by doing this of approaching your specific issues clinical depression, stress and anxiety, pain. But even without them, you can learn to apply these skills in your daily life. Here are some ideas:

See if you can figure out where your thoughts are going, what self-talk is taking over. Typically it concerns some disasterization that someone will be truly upset, that my boss will discharge me, that my discomfort will never ever go away, that I require to discover the best response to my concern in order to really feel far better?

Is there an actual issue that I require to take care of?

There is sensible anxiousness actual troubles, actual pain, depression from really feeling caught in your work and also illogical kinds. I'm depressed because I hate my job, but at my age I understand that I most likely can not find anything that will pay.

If there is a real trouble, you intend to take action: Currently send a text or email or call to your partner concerning the pick-up timetable; take the Advil for your back as well as skip your workouts tomorrow; go ahead as well as browse the web to see what could be in fact out there in regards to possible work, or set up a meeting with your supervisor to discuss methods of improving your day-to-day work tasks.

The secret below is a decisive activity. Do not dither by waiting till you speak with your companion, by browsing the web and also looking endlessly regarding various other factors your discomfort my be flaring, by crafting the perfect e-mail to your manager about your job, or chatting on your own out of seeking work.

If your problem is irrational

If you can't determine a specific issue and/or you can not discover a certain reason, or if they are clearly unreasonable you're stressed that you'll get sick because you touched the doorknob at the workplace, that you'll get lacked the church because you didn't volunteer for that committee, that you'll wind up in a wheelchair because of your neck and back pain this has to do with calming yourself down.

Here you can do journaling, drawing up what illogical thoughts are undergoing your mind, and then involving your rational mind as well as creating what is rational that you likely not get ill, run out of the church, not end up in a mobility device. As well as if you don't wish to write, deliberately speak to on your own similarly. You can also decrease your emotional stress my doing some workout, deep breathing, taking part in some mindful activities like cooking, by sidetracking on your own by playing a video game. Once again, the trick is an activity with the concentrate on soothing on your own down, as opposed to enabling on your own to go the rabbit-hole of searching for the ideal solution to your problem or disasterizing.

Criticism of Cognitive Behavior Modification

Some patients recommend that while they identify that certain ideas are not sensible or healthy and balanced, just coming to be conscious of these ideas does not make it simple to modify them. CBT does not have a tendency to concentrate on potential underlying unconscious resistances to transform as high as other approaches such as psychoanalytic psychiatric therapy.

It is necessary to keep in mind that CBT does not simply include identifying these thought patterns; it is concentrated on utilizing a wide variety of approaches to aid customers to conquer these thoughts. Such strategies might include journaling, role-playing, leisure strategies, and also mental diversions.

Cognitive-behavior treatment can be an effective treatment option for a series of psychological issues. Seek advice from with your doctor if you really feel that you may profit from this kind of therapy

DIALECTICAL BEHAVIOR THERAPY(DBT).

Dialectical behavior therapy (DBT) is a thorough cognitive-behavioral treatment. It intends to treat people who see little or no renovation with various other treatment models. This therapy concentrates on problem-solving and also acceptance-based techniques. It operates within a structure of dialectical approaches. The term dialectical describes the processes that bring contrary principles together such as adjustment and also approval.

Licensed experts of DBT supply approval and support to individuals in therapy. A lot of the people they deal with have actually conditions referred to as "hard to deal with." They work to establish methods for attaining goals, improving well-being, and impacting lasting positive change.

WHAT IS DIALECTICAL BEHAVIOR THERAPY?

Presently, DBT is utilized to treat individuals with persistent or extreme psychological health issues. Problems DBT deals with consist of self-harm, consuming and also food issues, dependency, and posttraumatic tension, along with borderline personality. DBT was initially developed to treat people who had chronic suicidal ideas as signs and symptoms of borderline character.

DBT can be made use of in a range of mental health setups. It incorporates the following five parts:

DBT gives chances for the development of existing skills. In treatment, 4 basic skill collections are instructed.

DBT therapists use various strategies to urge the transfer of finding out skills throughout all settings. A therapist may ask the individual in treatment to speak with a partner concerning a conflict.

Inspirational enhancement. DBT uses customized behavior therapy plans to decrease problematic behaviors that could negatively influence the quality of life. Therapists may use self-monitoring monitoring sheets so sessions can be adjusted to deal with the most serious problems.

Capacity and inspirational improvement of therapists. Since DBT is often given to people that experience chronic, severe, and also intense mental wellness problems, specialists obtain a great deal of guidance as well as support to stop things like vicarious traumatization or fatigue. Treatment-team meetings are held regularly to offer therapists an area to obtain and give assistance, training, as well as medical support.

Structuring of the setting. An objective of therapy is often to make certain favorable, flexible actions are strengthened throughout all ecological settings. If somebody gets involved in multiple treatment programs within one company, the specialist might make certain each program was established up to enhance all the positive abilities as well as actions found out.

The standard type of DBT is composed of private treatment, skills training team, phone training, as well as a specialist examination team. Those in basic DBT go to therapy as well as a skills training group weekly. Phone mentoring is additionally a vital part of DBT.

The issues encountered by lots of who participate in DBT can be complex and also extreme. As a result of this, a consultation group is considered important for DBT providers. The team is made up of team leaders as well as specific specialists. It can offer inspiration, therapy, and assistance to the specialists dealing with tough issues.

DEVELOPMENT AND ALSO HISTORY

DBT was created by Marsha Linehan in the 1970s. She established DBT through her work with two psychological health populaces: individuals with persistent ideas of suicide as well as individuals identified with a borderline personality disorder. Linehan was fascinated by the building online reputation of cognitive behavior treatment (CBT).

Individuals experienced change-focused treatments as revoking. These feelings typically caused withdrawal from therapy, hostility towards therapists, or a variation of both extremes.

When specialists pressed for modification, participants responded in anger. When specialists enabled a subject change, individuals responded with heat as well as favorable responses.

As a result of the intensity of crisis-related scenarios, specialists invested a bargain of time dealing with safety problems, such as self-destructive ideas or gestures, hostility and risks toward the therapist, or self-injurious actions. Commonly, little time was left to show coping skills or address behavioral functioning.

After evaluating these issues, Linehan developed numerous adjustments to CBT. These directly dealt with the demands of the populace. Acceptance-based methods were included to make certain individuals really felt sustained and confirmed prior to they were asked to concentrate on change. Furthermore, dialectics were incorporated to permit therapists and also participants in treatment to focus on the synthesis of polar opposites, such as approval and adjustment. This helped them to avoid ending up being entrapped in patterns of severe position-taking.

Given that then, the technique of DBT has grown in appeal. Over the last several years, a terrific offer of research has sustained the efficiency of DBT.

DBT THEORY

3 significant academic structures combine to form the basis for DBT These are a behavioral science biosocial design of the development of chronic mental wellness problems, the mindfulness method of Zen Buddhism, and the philosophy of dialectics.

The biosocial concept attempts to discuss how problems associated with borderline character create. The concept assumes that some individuals are born with a tendency towards psychological vulnerability. Settings that lack strong structure and security can increase a person's adverse emotional reactions. They can likewise affect patterns of interaction that become devastating. These patterns can hurt relationships as well as operating across all settings. They might frequently cause self-destructive actions and/or a medical diagnosis of borderline personality.

DBT draws mindfulness strategies from Zen Buddhism to use here-and-now clearheadedness. This may assist individuals in treatment objectively and also comfortably evaluate situations. Mindfulness training enables individuals to take stock of their existing experience, evaluate the realities, and also concentrate on one thing at once.

They pull from both extremes of an issue. Therapists make use of dialectics to help people accept the parts of themselves they do not like.

PHASES As Well As OBJECTIVES IN DBT.

Because DBT was originally intended for people with suicidal propensities as well as severe emotional issues, treatment happens in phases. DBT entails the adhering to 4 stages:

Phase 1. The focus of this phase is stabilizing. Individuals in therapy might be taking care of points like self-destructive ideas, self-harm, or addiction. They frequently report a sensation like they are at an all-time low point in their lives. Therapy is centered on security and situation intervention. The goal of this phase is to aid people to achieve some control over troublesome behaviors.

Phase 2. In this phase, habits are extra stable, but mental health and wellness issues may still be present. Psychological pain is generally brought to the surface. Stressful experiences are securely explored. The objective of this phase is for people in therapy to experience their psychological pain instead of silencing or hiding it.

Phase 3. This stage focuses on enhancing the quality of life via the upkeep of progress and also practical goal-setting. The objective of this stage is to promote happiness and also stability.

Phase 4.Throughout this phase, specialists support individuals in progressing their lives to the next level. The objective of this stage is to assist people in accomplishing and also keeping an ongoing capacity for joy as well as success.

HOW EFFECTIVE IS DBT?

Findings from numerous research studies show the efficiency of DBT. It may be specifically effective in dealing with borderline individuality concerns, posttraumatic stress and anxiety, self-harm, and suicidality.

A controlled test performed in an inpatient setting by Bohus et al. (2004) located individuals in therapy who got 3 months of DBT enhanced at a higher rate than those who got therapy as usual.

According to the SAMHSA National Registry of Evidence-based Programs as well as Practices, several controlled trials and independent research studies discovered one year of DBT reduced the circumstances of self-harming habits at a better rate than alternative treatments. One such research study reported that individuals who got DBT had just.55 incidents of self-injurious behavior over one month, contrasted to 9.33 events amongst those that obtained treatment as usual.

A research study performed by Linehan et al. (2006) suggests DBT may be effective in lowering self-destruction attempts. This research study reported those who got DBT were half as likely to attempt self-destruction. They had less psychological hospitalizations and also were much less most likely to leave therapy compared to those that received psychotherapy from experts considered experts in dealing with suicide as well as self-harm.

CERTIFICATION REQUIREMENTS FOR DBT

Some psychological health and wellness specialists offering DBT are not certified by the Linehan Board of Accreditation. The DBT-LBC program is the only developer-approved treatment program in the USA. Various other programs might not give practitioners with the essential training to supply DBT successfully. Therapy from a carrier who is not appropriately certified may merely be unsuccessful however might likewise cause damage.

DBT is a sort of therapy currently in high need. Numerous experts might wish to provide this therapy in their technique. It is necessary for all specialists that want to provide DBT to obtain certification via the DBT-LBC program.

Experts interested in becoming certified have to relate to taking an exam. The examination is based upon Linehan's training guidebook and also abilities training handbook. Those that pass are after that needed to submit first a therapy concept for a person they desire to treat with DBT Afterwards, they need to send 3 videotapes of successive therapy sessions with that said exact same person. If this finished Work Item adheres to DBT requirements, and the professional has shown the ability to successfully offer DBT, the expert can obtain accreditation as an Individual Specialist in DBT.

CRITICISMS As Well As RESTRICTIONS OF DBT.

A considerable body of research recommends DBT is an efficient treatment for several psychological health concerns. Yet there are a couple of objections as well as restrictions.

Much of the readily available study on the efficiency of DBT included little sample dimensions as well as focused on a particular sector of the psychological wellness population. Critics suggest more studies ought to be done to figure out if DBT functions well for those with varied or complex psychological wellness concerns.

DBT utilizes a thorough handbook and also needs strength training to implement. In several of the research studies where DBT was discovered to be reliable, the carriers implementing the DBT therapy were doctoral-level trainees or higher.

Numerous of the DBT study tests lasted up to a year. Due to the persistent nature of the conditions treated, the field can profit from even more research gauging treatment gains long after the management of DBT.

How DBT's Crisis Survival Abilities Aid

Have you ever seemed like your emotions are so frustrating they will never ever support? Possibly you have an intense impulse to return to risky or harmful behaviors to make on your own really feel better. Dialectical behavior therapy (DBT) has a whole component that focuses on situation survival abilities. These are abilities that aid you hang tough, or cope, when feelings are frustrating. It does not make the feeling vanish, but these abilities can aid you in making it through the strength of these emotions.

Below is a quick review of DBT's dilemma survival abilities.

DISTRACTION

These strategies are used to distract on your own from upsetting thoughts, sensations, or scenarios that feel frustrating. The acronym "APPROVES" can aid with recall in the minute.

Activities: Do something. Read, play a sport, or clean.

Contributing: Do something kind for another person. Put the recipes away, write a thank-you note, volunteer your time.

Contrasts: Compare your situation to another person's. This can assist move your focus far from your situation.

Emotions: Making on your own experience a various emotion can assist distract you. Enjoying amusing on the internet video clips, paying attention to love songs, or catching up on your favored daytime drama are all examples of just how you can distract yourself from overwhelming emotions.

You can use a timer to set a limit on your ideas or kind it all out in an email draft (or go "old college" and compose it on paper), and put it away so you do not concentrate on it for the time being. When you feel a lot more able to hang in there, go back as well as address whatever it is you pressed away.

Ideas: Distract on your own with other ideas that make it challenging to consider anything else. Say the alphabet in reverse, the count below 100 by 3s or 7s, or do a crossword or Sudoku puzzle.

Feelings: Magnify various other physical feelings. Eat a strong mint, family pet your pet dog, or squeeze a tension round.

SELF-SOOTHE WITH SIX SENSES

These approaches can aid you to feel much better and in control by using your five senses (and also a sixth:

motion) to ground you to this person, area, circumstance, as well as time.

Vision: Take a look at images that put you in an excellent mood, or go to a lovely location as well as admire the sights face to face. These can be connected to loved ones, nature, pets, or much more.

Hearing: Listen to unwinding songs or the noises around you.

Odor: Discover scents that relax you. Lavender is a strong go-to if you need help getting going.

Taste: Drink or eat something relaxing, such as mint or organic tea. Concentrate on exactly how pleasant it tastes.

Touch: Touch something relaxing. Snuggle in your favorite covering or animal your pet cat.

Activity: Move. Dance, go with a run, or do some other workout.

Boost the moment

You can not always alter the reality something is occurring, however you can change the way you feel, believe, or react utilizing these abilities.

Images: Use led images, or perhaps your own creative imagination, to envision even more pleasurable outcomes or circumstances.

Significance: My mommy enjoys to claim "whatever occurs for a factor." Being able to recognize or recognize why something occurred, or its function, can help you feel better concerning the truth it is occurring.

Petition: You can either pray in the standard feeling or use this ability as a form of reflection or journaling. Basically, you can utilize petition as a way to link emotionally or assess past, current, and future conditions.

Relaxation: Delight in something relaxing. Most likely to the coastline, get a massage, and even rest.

One thing in the minute: Concentrate on one thing at that minute. You can concentrate on your breathing, the noises you hear, or the means your chair feels.

Trip: This can be an actual journey or a "mental getaway." If you can not leave the scene or you're incapable of taking a physical vacation, getaway in a publication or a motion picture.

Motivation: Usage favorable self-talk. Pin inspirational quotes on your Pinterest web page or create them in a journal. Assess how amazing you are. Assess what you're succeeding now.

PROS AND CONS

Taking into consideration the brief- as well as long-term advantages and disadvantages to a choice can be practical in making a decision exactly how to respond to a scenario or sensation.

Tip the scale

When managing severe emotions or prompts, these skills are made use of. Utilizing these techniques might assist in readjusting your body chemistry.

Temperature: Run great water over your internal lower arms or chew on ice to physically "loosen up" and also "cool off."

Intense workout: Do 20 leaping jacks, 10 push-ups, or run in location for 1 minute.

Paced breathing: Decrease as well as count your breaths. You can use "square breathing" (matter to 4 as you breathe in, hold for four counts, matter to 4 as you exhale, hold for 4 matters, repeat).

Modern muscle mass leisure: Concentrate on pressing one muscle, after that release. Go on to the following muscle mass team in your body. You can locate manuscripts online that stroll you via this or do it by yourself.

It is important to keep in mind that one ability could not be adequate depending on exactly how intense your emotion or desire is. Have a willing mindset as you offer these abilities a try, as well as companion with a therapist trained in DBT if you desire to support.

Favorable assumptions for teens in DPT team abilities training

Many people understand the spirited expression, "When you think, you make a butt out of you and me." Why is this? Due to the fact that presumptions are unverified beliefs. If you assume mistakenly, without making an effort to gather or verify your assumptions with qualified resources, it can hurt relationships. Nonetheless, presumptions can benefit the therapeutic process when everybody settles on the same favorable assumptions.

The adhering to are DBT's Therapy Assumptions for Teens in a Skills Educating Team. Agreeing to these presumptions is believed to be useful for teens, their caretakers, and the abilities trainers. The idea is to end up being more accepting, less judgmental, and to assume and also act even more dialectically (one of the core ideas of DBT).

Everybody in the team is doing the very best they can. People are acting, thinking, and also emoting the very best method they are qualified at this time. It SUSCEPTIBILITY that, with time and method, their "finest" will boost.

Every person in the team wishes to improve. People don't intend to remain sensation, behaving, or assuming the way they presently are. As humans, we are constantly aiming to grow and also create significant methods.

Everybody needs to do much better, and also be extra inspired to change. This presumption goes together with the first 2 assumptions. While people are doing the best they can and also want to improve, they need to do (or act) far better as well as raise their motivation in order to make these adjustments.

Individuals might not have actually caused all of their problems, however they need to fix them anyhow. The phrase "the best-laid plans oft go awry" applies right here. If a person rear-ends your vehicle, you may not have actually caused the accident or be thought about "liable," however you still need to identify just how you are most likely to fix your auto. The same concept puts on group members' experiences. Keep in mind: For teens, given that they are underage, they may require to connect to encouraging adults to assist fix problems that are beyond their control or ability to fix on their own.

The lives of group members hurt as they are presently being lived. The ordinary person experiences numerous difficulties. Nonetheless, if you consider the experiences that added to a group participant being suggested and also accepted to a DBT abilities training group, it would be absurd not to consider that life might be extra difficult and also excruciating right now.

Group participants need to learn and also practice brand-new actions in all vital circumstances in their lives. It's always incredible when a group participant can master a skill in the therapy or group space. If you aren't taking and using the abilities all the other hrs of the week you spend outside of these spaces, you aren't obtaining the most bang for your dollar. This implies practicing and reviewing your experience by utilizing these abilities in day-to-day live experiences.

There is no outright truth. This is a hard idea to realize and live. By valuing the validity of two viewpoints, also when they feel like polar opposites, individuals can find out to value and also regard each other. When members find out more about exactly how to assume and act even

more dialectically, this is an idea that is commonly
further gone over and also exercised.

Teenagers and their household members can not fail in
DBT. Usually, individuals in therapy and their
households are blamed for not being encouraged
enough, working hard enough, or attempting hard
sufficient.

WHAT IS SCHEMA THERAPY?

Schema Therapy (or more properly, Schema-Focused Cognitive Therapy) is an integrative approach to treatment that combines the most effective facets of cognitive-behavioral, experiential, psychoanalytic as well as social therapies right into one unified design. Schema-Focused Therapy has shown amazing lead to helping people to alter unfavorable (" maladaptive") patterns which they have actually lived with for a long time, also when various other approaches and also efforts they have attempted prior to having been largely not successful.

The Schema-Focused design was created by Dr. Jeff Young, that initially functioned carefully with Dr. Aaron Beck, the owner of Cognitive Therapy. While dealing with clients at the Facility for Cognitive Therapy at the University of Pennsylvania, Dr. Young and also his coworkers recognized a segment of individuals that had a problem in profiting from the basic method.

The schemas that are targeted in treatment are withstanding and also self-defeating patterns that typically start early in life. These patterns contain negative/dysfunctional ideas and also feelings, have been repeated and also specified upon, as well as posture obstacles for accomplishing one's objectives and getting one's demands met. Some instances of schema beliefs are: "I'm unlovable," "I'm a failing," "Individuals uncommitted regarding me," "I'm trivial," "Something negative is going to occur," "People will leave me," "I will never ever get my demands satisfied," "I will never ever be good enough," and so on.

Schemas are generally developed early in life (throughout youth or teenage years), they can likewise develop later on, in adulthood. These schemas are bolstered behaviorally through the coping styles of schema upkeep, schema avoidance, and schema settlement. The Schema-Focused design of therapy is created to aid the person to break these unfavorable patterns of reasoning, feeling as well as behaving, which is typically really solid, as well as to develop much healthier alternatives to change them.

Schema-Focused Therapy contains 3 phases. First is the evaluation phase, in which schemas are recognized during the initial sessions. Surveys might be utilized also to obtain a clear picture of the various patterns involved. Next comes the psychological awareness as well as the experiential phase, in which clients contact these schemas and also learn just how to find them when they are operating in their everyday life. Thirdly, the behavioral adjustment stage comes to be the emphasis, during which the client is actively involved in changing negative, regular ideas and actions with brand-new, healthy cognitive and behavioral alternatives.

ABANDONMENT/ INSTABILITY (AB).

The perceived instability or unreliability of those available for support and link. Entails the sense that better halves will not be able to proceed to supply emotional support, connection, strength, or functional defense because they are uncertain as well as psychologically unstable (e.g., angry outbursts), unreliable, or unevenly present; because they will certainly die imminently; or due to the fact that they will certainly abandon the person in favor of somebody much better.

SKEPTICISM/ ABUSE (MA).

The expectation that will certainly hurt, abuse, humiliate, rip off, exist, manipulate, or capitalize. Typically involves the perception that the injury is deliberate or the result of severe as well as unjustified carelessness. May consist of the sense that a person always winds up being ripped off about others or "getting the short end of the stick.".

EMOTIONAL DEPRIVATION (ED).

The expectation that one's wish for a regular level of emotional support will certainly not be properly satisfied by others. The three significant forms of deprival are: A. Deprivation of Nurturance: Lack of focus, heat, love, or companionship.

DEFECTIVENESS/ EMBARASSMENT (DS).

The sensation that one is defective, bad, undesirable, inferior, or invalid in important areas; or that a person would certainly be unlovable to significant others if revealed. May involve hypersensitivity to blame, being rejected, and also objection; self-consciousness, contrasts, and also instability around others; or a sense of pity pertaining to one's regarded flaws. These problems may be private (e.g., narcissism, mad impulses, undesirable libidos) or public (e.g., unfavorable physical appearance, social awkwardness).

SOCIAL SECLUSION/ ALIENATION (SI).

The feeling that a person is isolated from the remainder of the world, various from other people, and/or not part of any kind of team or area.

RELIANCE/ INEXPERIENCE (DI).

The idea that one is not able to take care of one's day-to-day duties in a competent manner, without considerable aid from others (e.g., take care of oneself, solve daily problems, exercise profundity, take on brand-new jobs, make good choices). Commonly offers as vulnerability.

SUSCEPTIBILITY TO DAMAGE OR DISEASE (VH).

Exaggerated anxiety that imminent disaster will certainly strike at any moment and that one will be unable to stop it. Anxieties focus on one or more of the following: (A) Medical Catastrophes: e.g., cardiac arrest, AIDS; (B) Emotional Disasters: e.g., freaking out; (C): Exterior Catastrophes: e.g., elevators falling down, victimized by crooks, aircraft accidents, earthquakes.

ENMESHMENT/ UNTAUGHT SELF (EM).

Excessive emotional involvement and also distance with several significant others (commonly parents), at the expense of full individuation or regular social advancement. Typically involves the idea that at the very least among the enmeshed people can not survive or enjoy without the constant support of the various other. May also include feelings of being smothered by, or integrated with, others OR insufficient individual identification. Typically experienced as a feeling of emptiness as well as stumbling, having no instructions, or in extreme cases questioning one's existence.

FAILING (FA).

The idea that has fallen short, will inevitably fail, or is essentially poor relative to one's peers, in areas of success (school, career, sporting activities, etc.). It usually entails beliefs that a person is dumb, inefficient, untalented, ignorant, reduced in status, less effective than others, etc.

PRIVILEGE/ GRANDIOSITY (ET).

The idea that transcends to other individuals; entitled to special legal rights and privileges; or not bound by the policies of reciprocity that assist regular social communication. Frequently involves persistence that a person must be able to have or do whatever one desires, despite what is sensible, what others take into consideration sensible, or the price to others; OR an overstated focus on superiority (e.g., being amongst the most successful, popular, rich)-- in order to accomplish power or control (not primarily for interest or approval). Sometimes consists of too much competitiveness towards, or supremacy of, others: insisting one's power, compeling one's perspective, or controlling the actions of others in accordance with one's own wishes -without empathy or concern for others' demands or feelings.

INSUFFICIENT SELF-DISCIPLINE/ SELF-DISCIPLINE (IS).

Pervasive problem or refusal to work out adequate self-constraint as well as irritation resistance to attain one's personal goals, or to limit the too much expression of one's emotions and also impulses. In its milder form, the person presents with an exaggerated emphasis on discomfort-avoidance: preventing pain, dispute, overexertion, conflict, or duty - at the expense of personal gratification, commitment, or honesty.

SUBJUGATION (SB).

Excessive giving up of control to others since one feels pushed - typically to stay clear of retaliation, abandonment, or anger. The 2 significant kinds of subjugation are: A. Subjugation of Demands: Suppression of one's choices, choices, and also needs. Normally entails the assumption that one's very own wishes, opinions, as well as sensations are not legitimate or essential to others.

SELF-SACRIFICE (SS).

Excessive focus on willingly meeting the needs of others in day-to-day scenarios, at the cost of one's very own gratification. Occasionally leads to a sense that one's own requirements are not being effectively satisfied and to the resentment of those who are taken treatment of.

APPROVAL-SEEKING/ RECOGNITION-SEEKING (AS).

Excessive emphasis on acquiring authorization, recognition, or focus from other people, or suitable in, at the expense of developing a true and also secure sense of self. One's feeling of esteem is reliant mainly on the responses of others instead than on one's very own all-natural inclinations.

NEGATIVENESS/ PESSIMISM (NP).

A pervasive, lifelong focus on the adverse elements of life (discomfort, death, loss, frustration, dispute, sense of guilt, bitterness, unresolved problems, potential errors, dishonesty, points that might go incorrect, etc.) while reducing or overlooking the positive or favorable elements. Typically consists of an exaggerated assumption - in a large array of job, financial, or social situations - that points will eventually go seriously wrong, or that elements of one's life that seem to be going well will eventually drop apart.

EMOTIONAL RESTRAINT (EI).

The too much inhibition of spontaneous activity, feeling, or interaction - generally to avoid displeasure by others, feelings of shame, or blowing up of one's impulses. One of the most common areas of restraint entail: (a) inhibition of rage & aggressiveness; (b) inhibition of favorable impulses (e.g., happiness, affection, sex-related excitement, play); (c) problem expressing susceptability or connecting easily regarding one's feelings, demands, and so on; or (d) too much emphasis on rationality while disregarding feelings.

UNRELENTING STANDARDS/
HYPERCRITICALNESS (United States).

The underlying idea that one needs to aim to meet very high internalized standards of habits and also efficiency, typically to avoid criticism. Unrelenting criteria generally offer as: (a) perfectionism, excessive focus to detail, or an underestimate of just how good one's very own performance is relative to the norm; (b) rigid guidelines and also "shoulds" in lots of locations of life, consisting of unrealistically high moral, honest, social, or religious mandates; or (c) obsession with time as well as performance, so that even more can be accomplished.

PUNITIVENESS (PU).

The belief that people should be harshly penalized for making mistakes. Involves the tendency to be upset, intolerant, punitive, and also impatient with those people (including oneself) who do not satisfy one's assumptions or criteria. Normally includes problem forgiving mistakes in oneself or others, as a result of hesitation to consider mitigating scenarios, permit human imperfection, or empathize with feelings.

What are the core needs of a child?

One of the biggest factors in the development of schemas is not having your core emotional demands met as a kid.

This core requires to consist of:

a feeling of security and also being safely connected to others

a sense of self-identity and also freedom

the flexibility to reveal how you feel and ask of what you need from others

the capacity to play as well as being spontaneous

risk-free, age-appropriate limits and borders

On top of that, four sorts of adverse experiences can likewise add to the growth of schemas. These include:

Unfulfilled demands. When you do not obtain affection from caregivers or stop working to have other core emotional needs met, this can take place.

Traumatization or victimization. This defined a scenario when you experienced abuse, injury, or similar distress.

Overindulgence or lack of limitations. In this scenario, your parents might have been overinvolved or overprotective. They might not have established the correct limits for you.

Careful identification and also internalization. This describes the way you soak up a few of your mom's and dads' actions or perspectives. You might identify with several of these and also internalize others. Some may develop into schemas, while others develop into settings, also called dealing methods.

What kind of coping designs do schemas develop?

In schema treatment, your reactions to schemas are referred to as dealing designs. These can involve habits, feelings, or ideas. They establish as a means of preventing the frustrating and unpleasant feelings experienced as a result of a particular schema.

Coping designs can be valuable in childhood years, as they provide a method of survival. Yet in the adult years, they can enhance schemas.

There aren't any solid policies about which schemas bring about particular dealing styles. Your coping design may be based on your total character or perhaps the dealing styles you learned from your parents.

They also vary from person to person. Two people could reply to the exact same schema with the exact same style in extremely different methods. Likewise, two individuals with the same schema might likewise respond with 2 separate styles.

Your own coping design can likewise alter in time, although you're still handling the very same schema.

The three primary dealing styles freely correlate with the fight-or-flight or freeze response:

Give up

This involves providing and accepting a schema into it. It normally results in behavior that enhances or proceeds the schema pattern.

For instance, if you surrender to a schema that developed as a result of psychological forget as a child, you may later on find yourself in a relationship entailing psychological overlook.

Avoidance

This involves trying to live without activating the schema. You may prevent tasks or circumstances that could perhaps cause them or make you feel prone.

Preventing your schema may leave you more vulnerable to compound use, risky or uncontrollable actions, as well as other habits that give a distraction.

Overcompensation

This entails attempting to combat a schema by acting in complete resistance to it. This might feel like a healthy and balanced response to a schema, however overcompensation typically goes too far.

It often leads to actions or actions that appear aggressive, requiring, aloof, or excessive somehow. This can take a toll on your partnerships with others.

What are schema settings?

In schema treatment, a mode is a short-term frame of mind that consists of both your present mood as well as how you're handling it.

To put it simply, your setting is a mix of energetic schemas and coping designs. Settings can be useful (flexible) or purposeless (maladaptive).

Schema settings aid specialists group schemas with each other so they can address them as a single state of mind, rather than private attributes.

Schema settings are split into four categories:

Youngster modes are characterized by childlike sensations and behaviors.

Dysfunctional coping settings are used to avoid emotional distress yet wind up reinforcing the schema.

Useless parent modes are internalizations of critical, requiring, or harsh adult voices.

The healthy grown-up setting represents your healthy, functional self. This setting can aid in regulating the various other modes by establishing limitations and also countering the results of other settings.

What are the goals of schema therapy?

In schema treatment, you'll work with your therapist to:

begin as well as determine healing schemas

determine as well as attend to coping designs that get in the way of psychological requirements

change patterns of feelings and also actions that arise from schemas

learn how to get your core emotional demands met in healthy, flexible methods

learn exactly how to cope (in a healthy and balanced way) with aggravation as well as distress when specific demands can't be met

Ultimately, all of this will certainly help you create a strong, healthy grown-up mode. A strong healthy and balanced adult mode can assist recover as well as control other settings and also aid in maintaining you from being bewildered by their impacts.

What strategies are made use of?

Schema specialists might use a number of strategies throughout therapy. Specific methods may function much better for some individuals as well as schemas than others. If a specific method doesn't benefit you, make certain to let your therapist understand.

On that note, keep in mind that your relationship with your specialist is an integral part of schema treatment. There are two essential principles that appear in a lot of the techniques utilized in schema treatment. When you really feel comfortable and secure with your therapist, both work best.

These principles are:

Compassionate confrontation. Your therapist verifies the schemas showing up in treatment, offering understanding and also empathy while aiding you to recognize the value of change.

Minimal reparenting. Your therapist assists satisfy psychological requirements that weren't met in youth by providing safety and security, regard, and also empathy. "Restricted" merely means your specialist ensures this reparenting aligns with ethical criteria for mental health professionals.

Normally, these ideas are carried out with methods that fall under 4 groups:

Emotive

Stirring strategies include utilizing emotions to counter schemas. They assist you in totally experience feelings as well as share them in the safety of the treatment. Usual emotive strategies consist of led images and role-playing.

Interpersonal

Social strategies aid you analyze your partnerships to recognize means schemas affect them.

Seeing exactly how responses and schemas play out in therapy can help you reveal similar patterns in your life. This might include generating a partner or friend to a therapy session.

Cognitive

Cognitive strategies involve identifying and testing harmful thought patterns that arise from schemas. You'll collaborate with your specialist to evaluate life experiences for proof that contradicts the schema or supports.

This could be done through the use of flashcards or structured conversations in which you'll speak both in favor of and also against a schema.

Behavior

Behavior methods aid you learn to make favorable, healthy and balanced selections by transforming the habits patterns that arise from your coping design.

To change behavioral patterns, you could service communication skills with role-playing or talk via trouble as well as remedy with your specialist. They may also give you some workout to do in between sessions.

What are the constraints of schema treatment?

Schema therapy shows assurance as a treatment for many psychological wellness concerns, consisting of consuming problems and anxiety.

Most of the existing study has actually looked at the function of schema treatment in dealing with borderline personality disorder and also various other personality disorders.

So far, the results are appealing. As an example, a 2014 controlled trial concluded that schema therapy might be much more reliable for treating personality disorders.

Schema treatment has actually just been around given that the 1980s. This is a relatively short quantity of time on the planet of psychology. Because of this, there aren't several top quality, lasting researches about its results.

While the existing research is appealing, most experts agree that there's a requirement for more tests as well as research.

Compared to other kinds of therapy, schema treatment can additionally be a lasting dedication. You might require to undertake schema therapy for many years. This can additionally come to be quite pricey if you don't have an insurance policy.

Just how can I attempt schema treatment?

It's a little bit harder to locate a schema therapist than various other sorts of specialists, especially in the USA, but resources are out there.

The International Society of Schema Therapy has a directory site that lists officially educated schema therapists.

You can also attempt browsing basic therapist databases, including the American Psychological Organization's specialist finder.

Try to seek therapists that provide CBT. Schema therapy draws heavily from this strategy, so some CBT therapists may have some experience with schema therapy or its core principles.

Since schema treatment might set you back greater than various other kinds of mental health and wellness therapy, it's an excellent concept to ask therapists regarding expense, whether they approve insurance policy, and also other monetary issues you might have.

PSYCHODYNAMIC THERAPY

Psychodynamic treatment, additionally called insight-oriented therapy, concentrates on subconscious procedures as they are manifested in a person's existing behavior. The objectives of psychodynamic therapy are a client's self-awareness as well as an understanding of the impact of the past on present habits. In its quick form, a psychodynamic method allows the client to analyze unsolved problems and signs that emerge from past useless connections and materialize themselves in the requirement and also wish to abuse compounds.

Several different methods to brief psychodynamic psychotherapy have actually developed from psychoanalytic theory and also have been medically related to a large range of mental problems. There is a body of study that normally sustains the efficacy of these techniques.

Psychodynamic treatment is the earliest of the modern treatments. The material offered in this chapter gives a fast look at the efficiency and also the complicated nature of this kind of therapy.

History of Psychodynamic Therapy

The concept supporting psychodynamic treatment came from as well as is informed by psychoanalytic theory. There are four major institutions of psychoanalytic theory, each of which has actually influenced psychodynamic treatment. The four colleges are: Freudian, Ego Psychology, Item Relations, and also Self Psychology.

Freudian psychology is based upon the theories initially created by Sigmund Freud in the very early part of this century as well as is in some cases referred to as the drive or architectural version. The essence of Freud's theory is that hostile and also sex-related energies coming from the id (or unconscious) are modulated by the vanity, which is a set of features that moderates between the id as well as outside truth. Defense reaction is buildings of the ego that run to reduce pain and to preserve psychic stability. The superego, developed throughout latency (in between age 5 and also adolescence), operates to manage id drives with sense of guilt.

Vanity Psychology stems from Freudian psychology. Its advocates focus their work on enhancing and also keeping vanity features according to the demands of reality. Ego Psychology emphasizes the person's ability for reality, defense, and adaptation screening.

According to this theory, human beings are constantly shaped in relation to the substantial others surrounding them. Our battles and also goals in life focus on preserving relationships with others, while at the same time distinguishing ourselves from others.

Self Psychology was started by Heinz Kohut, M.D., in Chicago during the 1950s. Kohut observed that the self describes an individual's understanding of his experience of his self, including the existence or absence of a sense of self-confidence. The self is regarded in connection with the establishment of borders as well as the differentiation of self from others (or the absence of differentiations and also boundaries).

Each of the 4 colleges of psychoanalytic concept provides distinct concepts of personality development, psychopathology formation, and also adjustment; methods through which to conduct treatment; as well as signs as well as contraindications for treatment. Psychodynamic therapy is differentiated from psychoanalysis in numerous details, including the reality that psychodynamic treatment need not consist of all analytic strategies as well as is not performed by psychoanalytically trained analysts. Psychodynamic therapy is also performed over a much shorter time period as well as with much less frequency than psychoanalysis.

Intro to Short Psychodynamic Therapy

The recovery as well as change procedure visualized in long-term psychodynamic therapy generally requires a minimum of 2 years of sessions. This is because the objective of therapy is frequently to transform an element of one's identity or personality or to integrate essential developing learning missed while the client was stuck at an earlier phase of emotional growth.

Practitioners of short psychodynamic treatment believe that some modifications can happen via a more fast process or that an initial brief intervention will certainly begin a continuous procedure of change that does not need the constant participation of the therapist. A central idea in brief therapy is that there must be one significant focus for the therapy instead than the more traditional psychoanalytic technique of permitting the client to connect freely and review inapplicable problems. In brief therapy, the main emphasis is created during the preliminary assessment procedure, occurring during the initial session or 2.

The number of specialists who exercise a special form of psychodynamic treatment today is a tiny percentage of psychotherapists. Lots of psychotherapists utilize components of psychodynamic concepts, nonetheless, in their solution of a client's problems, while employing other sorts of mental strategies (usually, cognitive-behavioral strategies) to influence adjustment in the individual.

Objectives of Psychodynamic Therapy

The main goals of psychodynamic therapy are to improve the customer's self-awareness and foster understanding of the customer's thoughts, sensations, and beliefs in regard to their past experiences, particularly his or her experiences as a youngster (Haggerty, 2016). This is achieved by the therapist leading the client via the examination of unsettled disputes and considerable events in the customer's past.

The assumption in psychodynamic treatment is that persistent problems are rooted in the unconscious mind as well as has to be brought to light for catharsis to take place. Hence, the client needs to have the self-awareness to discover these subconscious patterns of thought and also an understanding of how these patterns came to be in order to handle them.

Psychodynamic Theory, Perspective, and Secret Principles

To truly understand the psychodynamic treatment, you need to return to its origins. While this type of treatment has changed over the last century, it is still built on the structures of a few of the earliest work in modern-day psychology.

In the late 19th century, Sigmund Freud was servicing his grand concept of the human mind as well as the theory of human development. His theories laid the foundation for decades of psychological research and also method. While many of these theories were at some point found to contravene tough evidence gotten through a clinical research study, they created the basis for psychodynamic concept and also sparked a vibrant brand-new institution of idea that still exists today, in a changed and updated type.

He proposed that the human mind is made up of 3 parts:

The id, which consists of impulse and also creates the basis of the unconscious mind;

The superego, or ethical element that houses our ideas of right and wrong;

The vanity, the mediator between the pet instinct of the id and the informed ethical thought of the superego.

Freud assumed that these parts grew out of particular phases in childhood year's advancement. He thought people are born with the id, develop the vanity as a kid, and also include the superego around the age of five. Freud's hypothesis led him to the rational conclusion (based upon his theory) that's individuality is securely rooted in their childhood year's experiences.

While Freud thought that each component created in each human, the advancement of each element could be dramatically influenced by one's atmosphere and family connections. These elements could contribute to the advancement of a healthy and balanced feeling of self and also effective functioning, or they could trigger the development of neuroses and inefficient or upsetting patterns of thought.

Whether the growth resulted in negative or positive patterns of ideas and also the idea, Freud held that which genuinely drives human habits is buried deep within the human mind, in what he termed the unconscious mind.

Freud theorized three levels of the mind:

The Unconscious: this degree is where our instincts, deeply held ideas, and also lots of patterns of idea and habits reside; we are not knowingly familiar with anything at this degree, yet Freud believed the components of the subconscious mind comprise the vast majority of who we are, what we want, as well as how we behave in order to get what we want.

The Subconscious or Preconscious: this level is between the conscious and unconscious, and can be phoned to awareness with a deliberate initiative from the individual;

the materials of this level are simply listed below the surface area of consciousness.

The Conscious: this is the level at which we are completely mindful; Freud believed this was the degree with the least specifying web content, the degree that makes up just a little bit of that we are.

Based on this concept, Freud insisted that to genuinely address our problems and also address our issues, we must dig deep into the subconscious level. This is where we store our unmentioned values, the beliefs we do not also understand we have, as well as the patterns of idea and also habits developed in our childhood years.

While psychodynamic concept has actually outgrown a number of Freud's simplified ideas about human nature, a lot of the assumptions that underlie the psychodynamic method are reminiscent of Freud's work:

The subconscious mind is one of the most effective vehicle drivers of human habits and also feeling;

No behavior lacks reason all behavior is established;

Childhood years experiences exert a substantial influence on thoughts, emotions, and actions as an adult;

Important problems throughout youth development shape our total personality as adults (Freud, 1899).

Freud's concepts directly sustain the approaches of psychoanalysis, but likewise assist in developing the basis of psychodynamic concept and notify the approaches and methods used in today's psychodynamic therapy.

Psychoanalysis: The Freudian Approach

While psychoanalysis and modern-day psychodynamic treatment grew from the very same source, there are numerous important distinctions between both forms of therapy.

The timeline as well as the period of psychoanalysis are much more intensive than contemporary psychodynamic therapy. Psychoanalysis is typically conducted in 2 to 5 sessions weekly, lasting a number of years (McLeod, 2014).

Second, the physical layout of the office or treatment area is substantial-- in psychoanalysis, the client (or person, as they are typically called) lies on his or her back on a sofa while the therapist sits behind them, out of their view. In modern psychodynamic treatment, it is a lot more common for therapists and clients to deal with each other, or at least continue to be in the other's field of view.

Third, the relationship between specialist and client/patient is far more imbalanced than in modern psychodynamic treatments. The placement of the therapist and client recommends a significant imbalance of power, with the specialist functioning as a remote as well as a separated specialist with strategies as well as understanding that will not be shared with the customer. At the same time, the client acts as a distressed supplicant that relies on the specialist for their expertise in teasing out the inefficient thoughts and also ideas that pester them (McLeod, 2014).

Several of the psychoanalytical methods have actually survived or been adjusted for modern-day usage, but this uneven partnership between therapist and client generally does not rollover to present psychodynamic therapy. The specialist's role has actually been changed over the last century to alter the pecking order and also give a much more equivalent setting for treatment.

Role of the Psychodynamic Specialist

Today, the role of the specialist in psychodynamic therapy is to deal with the client to discover the bases for their signs.

The therapist plays this role by urging the customer to speak about the emotions they are feeling as well as aiding the client to recognize recurring patterns in their actions, thoughts, as well as feelings. They can aid the client in locating the value of these patterns and also uncovering the results they apply upon the customer.

One of the most vital roles of the therapist is to penetrate the customer's past. Conversation of the client's youth as well as early life experiences will likely occupy a large part of psychodynamic sessions, as this form of therapy presumes these experiences have a considerable effect on the client's present concerns.

The specialist observes just how the customer communicates within the healing connection and also includes their very own insight into the client's relationship behaviors to the discussion. The psychodynamic concept holds that exactly how the customer acts in the partnership with the specialist usually mirrors just how they act in other connections, such as with a parent or other vital grownup from their childhood.

In general, the therapist's function is to aid the client in linking the dots between their previous experiences as well as their existing issues, and take advantage of their inner sources to attend to these problems.

Types of Psychodynamic Therapy

Throughout this item, I have actually described psychodynamic therapy as a single entity to make the discussion of psychodynamic therapies easier; but honestly composing, psychodynamic treatment is extra a category of therapies as opposed to a single type.

All of the therapies listed below are based on the very same overarching design of psychodynamic theory, yet they apply the tenets of this theory in different means.

1. Short Psychodynamic Therapy

The element of quick psychodynamic therapy that sets it apart from other kinds of psychodynamic treatments is right in the name: quick.

This type of treatment is normally carried out throughout just a couple of sessions, or even simply one session in many cases. In some cases a specific battling with particular trouble just requires to make a couple of important links to overcome that problem. For example, if a customer is dealing with acute stress and anxiety without any well-known source, the identification of an occasion or condition that generated this anxiety as well as a strategy for coping can be achieved in one session.

While the resolution of troubles ought to not be expected in one session for all those looking for treatment, there are several circumstances where recognizing as well as dealing with a specific issue can be a fairly brief financial investment.

The quick psychodynamic treatment has actually been put on situations like:

- Rape;

- Mishap (traffic, physical injury, etc.);.

- Act of terrorism;.

- Intense mental disruptions (like anxiety or
  depression);.

- Traumatic family members occasion (exploration of
  a trick, separation, and so on).

2. Psychodynamic Household Treatment

This form of psychodynamic therapy is practiced in the
context of a family, whether that family consists of two
adults in a charming relationship, a parent and also kid(
ren), grandchildren, brother or sisters and grandparents, a
standard extended family, or any type of mix of these
relative.

This treatment is generally fairly lasting (versus the much
shorter term household therapy based on CBT or IPT) and
also frequently is initiated by persistent troubles in the
family members (rather than a considerable occasion or the
emersion of a certain issue in the family).

Like other psychodynamic treatments, this type focuses on
unconscious procedures and unsolved disputes yet watches

them in the context of family member's relationships. The therapist will certainly lead the member of the family with an expedition of family member's history, particularly any kind of terrible family event.

Frequently, this type of treatment stresses the value of the grown-up members of the family exercising any conflicts with their very own moms and dads as a method to better comprehend the disputes with their partner(s) as well as the child(ren).

Psychodynamic family members therapy can help families to uncover and also address the deep-seated problems that give rise to household troubles, leading to a much healthier as well as happier family dynamic.

3. Psychodynamic Art/ Music Treatment

This non-traditional kind of psychodynamic therapy involves the expression of sensations and also emotions through art or songs.

Like other types of psychodynamic treatment, this treatment is non-structured and non-directive, allowing the client to lead the session. It does not need any type of imaginative or musical talent or ability, only that customers are able to utilize songs or art to express themselves.

Clients might display details items and also speak about the emotions they evoke, attach them to events from youth, or review the definition they locate in these pieces. Or, customers may generate a particular song or album that they feel they can relate to on a deep degree.

Customers can really create art or songs in the session. It doesn't need to be "great" art or music, it only requires to share the thoughts or feelings of the customers in a manner that makes sense to them.

With art and/or music, the therapist and client can construct an understanding and also form an important bond. They may locate that art and music are better approaches to deep communication than chatting.

This type of therapy may be especially well fit for those who are timid or otherwise discover it difficult to chat, as well as clients who are experiencing crippling anxiousness or worry which music or art can assist in relieving.

5 Psychodynamic Devices and also Strategies

Psychodynamic treatment depends less on exercises and activities than many various other sorts of therapy, yet there are some extremely important devices in the psychodynamic toolbox that enable the specialist to delve deep right into the unconscious mind with their customers.

The five tools and methods listed below are common techniques for lots of kinds of psychodynamic therapy.

1. Psychodynamic Diagnostic Manual (PDM).

The Diagnostic and Statistical Handbook, or DSM, is frequently referred to as the scientific psycho therapist's Scriptures. The DSM acts as a framework for understanding and also assessing actions within a therapeutic context.

Psychodynamic therapists as well as theorists often review the DSM's concentrate on visible signs as well as noninclusion of more subjective experiences as standards for medical diagnosis.

To fix this problem of dispute over diagnostic requirements, a Psychodynamic Diagnostic Guidebook (or

PDM) was launched in 2006 as an alternate or enhance to the DSM. Those practicing psychodynamic therapy may locate this guidebook to be more useful in diagnosing and treating their clients than the common DSM.

You can find out more concerning the PDM below.

2. Rorschach Inkblots.

While these unclear and also messy splotches of ink are carefully attached to Freudian psychoanalysis, they are also utilized in some types of psychodynamic treatment today.

The Rorschach Inkblot test appears to be a particularly misinterpreted device in the basic populace. Pop culture has made the test out to be either an end-all, be-all test of a person's personality, unique psychology, as well as forecaster of all manner of psychological health and wellness maladies, or an ineffective exercise in calling unnamable forms.

Actually, the Rorschach test is neither of these points. It can not illuminate your entire childhood years experience, however it is also not a worthless bit of trivia from a psychological age gone by.

The original Rorschach inkblots were developed in the very early 1900s by psychologist Hermann Rorschach (Framingham, 2016). At the time, a popular video game called Blotto entailed a set of inkblots that can be organized right into a rhyme or story or made use of in a round of charades. Rorschach saw that individuals diagnosed with schizophrenia reacted in different ways to these inkblots, and also started studying their use as a device for medical diagnosis and also conversation of signs and symptoms.

His job caused a set of 10 inkblot pictures that can be presented to a customer with the intention of predicting and observing based upon their responses to the photos.

To carry out the Rorschach examination, the therapist will certainly present each inkblot to the customer independently and also ask the client to define what they see. They are complimentary to utilize the photo as a whole, a piece of the photo, or even the empty space bordering the photo to create an analysis.

The specialist will take notes on the client's summaries as well as how they analyze the picture. They might likewise ask extra concerns to obtain the client to clarify on what they see.

While there is debate over how legitimate and reputable the outcomes of this test ought to be considered, several therapists find that they offer useful qualitative details about just how the client is really feeling and also just how they assume (Cherry, 2017). It has actually also been located to be somewhat effective in the diagnosis of assuming disorders (such as schizophrenia and also bipolar disorder). Those with these types of conditions have a tendency to see and also translate the images differently than those without such diagnoses.

The integral part of this examination is the procedure of interpretation and also description taken on by the customer, as opposed to any details material seen in the inkblots. Because of this, making use of this examination requires a highly trained professional to carry out, score, as well as interpret.

3. Freudian Slip

This might be the least formal (as well as possibly the very least employed) strategy in psychodynamic treatment, yet it is certainly not a dead principle.

A "Freudian slip" is additionally called a slip of the tongue or, a lot more formally, parapraxes. These slips refer to instances when we mean to claim something but accidentally allow "slip" one more, particularly when much deeper significance can be credited to this slip.

You could call it a Freudian slip when someone intends to state "That is your best suggestion yet!" Unintentionally states "That is your bust suggestion yet!" You may think that this person has a specific physiological feature in mind, or links the person they are addressing with claimed attribute.

Freud (and some subsequent psychodynamic philosophers) believed that these "accidental" slips of the tongue are not really unintended, yet actually reveal something meaningful regarding you. The Freudian concept holds that no habits are random or accidental; instead, every relocation you make and also every word you claim are established by your mind (conscious, subconscious, or unconscious) and your situations.

A psychodynamic therapist might pay unique focus to any such slides, whether they occur in session or are merely connected by the customer during a session, as well as find meaning in the word substitution. They might conclude that a slip is in fact a little piece of your subconscious finding its means to the surface, suggesting an unmet wish or unidentified organization in between 2 principles.

While most modern psychotherapists concur that Freudian slides are typically simply "slides," it's tough to say that a slip of the tongue can't periodically reveal an intriguing link in the audio speaker's mind.

4. Free Organization

Free association may be the solitary crucial and many made use of device for psychodynamic specialists. This technique is basic and typically reliable.

In the context of psychodynamic treatment, there are two definitions affixed to "totally free association:" a lot more main treatment technique of free association, as well as the general method of in-session discussion driven by the client's cost-free organization in between subjects.

The more official strategy entails the therapist reading a checklist of words as well as the customer responding immediately with the first word that comes to mind. This workout can clarify a few of the associations as well as links the customer has concealed deep below the surface area.

This strategy might not be as helpful to a customer who is resistant to the workout or to sharing intimate details with the specialist. Therapists need to not presume that a customer who pauses before responding is resistant-- it may suggest that the client is obtaining closer to a repressed or extremely substantial connection.

Complimentary association might prompt a particularly intense or brilliant memory of a terrible event, called abreaction. This can be incredibly stressful for the client, but it can also cause a healing experience of catharsis if the client seems to like it aided them to resolve a significant issue (McLeod, 2014).

Practicing this type of casual complimentary association guarantees that the specialist is not leading the client anywhere in certain which the client is moving authentically from one subject to the following. This is vital in psychodynamic treatment, as it is unlikely to get to the subconscious resources of emotional distress without adhering to the client's lead.

5. Fantasize Analysis

An additional vestige of Freudian therapy, this highly subjective method can verify helpful for some, although its effectiveness as a treatment method is not verified by means of the scientific technique.

Nonetheless, the performance of treatment can not constantly be measured and ordered by double-blind arbitrary control tests (RCTs), the gold criterion of study. Often it is virtually difficult to determine which components or modes of therapy produced success in treatment.

It remains in this ambiguous setting that some of those not-quite-established strategies can add to actual development for the client. While dream analysis can not be officially suggested as a trusted and also efficient device, it is not likely to trigger any type of harm and also should, for that reason, be left as much as the client as well as specialist whether to include it in the treatment regimen.

Dream evaluation is undertaken by talking about the client's dreams carefully. The therapist will certainly guide the customer through this discussion, asking concerns as well as pushing the customer to define the desire as well as keep in mind in as much detail as possible.

While Freud would virtually always find a repressed sexual urge or sex-related relevance in the unrealized content, today's dream interpreters have widened their scope of significance.

There are nearly many manner ins which specialists, instructors, counselors, and experts of the more magical arts take part in dream evaluation, none of which have actually been recognized as more beneficial or reliable than the others.

However, one popular approach to analyzing desires originates from a psychologist as well as writer Dr. Patrick McNamara. His concept of the dreaming process can be explored on an individual level, enabling the client to attempt to arrange via their own desires to locate meaning.

McNamara's recommended process of fantasizing is as follows:

Step One: The dreamer disentangles their consciousness from executive control/personal agency. Simply put, the daydreamer de-identifies with their normal self and also sets up a "liminal state"-- a state in which the dreamer is prepared to discover a brand-new identification.

Step Two: The dreamer relocates right into this liminal area, opening him- or herself approximately a world of possibilities in relation to their identification. This step is like taking off your normal "mask" and set it apart in expectancy of locating a new mask.

Tip Three: This step normally inhabits the most time as well as material of the dream, in which the daydreamer "tries on" a new identity. The daydreamer might be experiencing fear or anxiousness connected with losing their identity, and he or she might look to re-establish a sense of control by searching for an additional identity or an alternative sense of self.

Tip Four: The dreamer discovers a brand-new, transformed identity or resumes their old identification. McNamara believes we are searching for an extra unified feeling of self, however that we frequently locate an identification that consists of facets of our darker side (McNamara, 2017).

These actions are linked into 4 literary tropes that some think we make use of to make sense of the narratives we encounter and also experience: metonymy (separating the items of a narrative), synecdoche (restructuring those items into a new whole), allegory (comparison of the pieces or the whole with something acquainted), as well as irony (reflection of the brand-new whole).

Making use of these devices for comprehending the story, McNamara recommends we can use this process and also the literary tropes to analyze the definition of any type of desire or dream sequence (2017). Obviously, this method has not been verified through a scientific research study, yet you might find it handy however.

TRANSFERENCE-FOCUSED THERAPY (TFP).

Mostly created for individuals with a borderline character (BPD) diagnosis, transference-focused psychiatric therapy (TFP) functions to help individuals develop positive self-regard and also more constructive behaviors. TFP helps identify bothersome patterns of interaction or suicidal suggestions as they arise throughout a therapy session, as opposed to concentrating just on scenarios that develop outside of psychotherapy.

WHAT IS TRANSFERENCE-FOCUSED TREATMENT?

Transfer is the phenomenon in which an individual tasks emotions or expectations onto one more person, particularly their specialist. This usually takes place automatically as well as may be ignored unless it disrupts restorative progress. TFP, however, assumes transfer is a regular or predicted part of psychiatric therapy, and also utilizes it to break down harmful behavioral patterns.

As an example, a transference-focused therapist would vocally determine, or ask the person in treatment to recognize, examples of their habits that are happening promptly in the course of a treatment session. By shining a light on those bothersome communications when they occur, both specialists and customers can better identify and create favorable options for damaging or potentially harmful habits as it occurs.

WHAT TFP CONTAINER ASSIST WITH.

Most research study pertaining to TFP has evaluated its result on individuals who have a borderline individuality diagnosis. In several studies, TFP has effectively:.

Decreased common signs of BPD, such as impulsivity, self-harm, irritation, as well as temper.

Improved emotional guideline.

Reduced anxiousness as well as depressive signs and symptoms.

Improved social interactions.

Minimized suicidal ideation.

Some initial study additionally sustains the use of TFP for other mental health and wellness considerations such as narcissism. Since vanity as well as borderline can share some traits associated with social communications, TFP may be conveniently related to identifying comparable patterns in people with narcissism. Specialists utilizing TFP with individuals who have conceited personality type may require to be more mindful of resistance to treatment as well as a tendency towards attrition in these populaces.

HOW DOES TFP WORK?

TFP is based upon a twice-weekly therapy method that utilizes things relationships theory to boost as well as change ingrained behavioral patterns that may be devastating or undesirable. Object relations concept is the belief that human beings are motivated by social communication and also connections with various other people than by sex or aggressiveness. By attending to behaviors from the standpoint that all people essentially intend to enhance relations with others, therapists focus on the method a person can make an enduring therapy, as opposed to on their regarded pathologies.

The International Society for Transference-Focused Psychiatric therapy expresses two ideas that assist the practice of TFP:.

Treatment counts on the acknowledgment of signs as interior variables and also emotional states, not as manifestations noticeable to the naked eye.

Both customers and also specialists continuously establish and also hone their awareness of the customer's signs or troublesome behaviors throughout the program of therapy, not just throughout assessment or the preliminary stage of therapy.

TFP motivates the person in treatment to take obligation for their actions and actions through the understanding that while the diagnosis of a personality disorder may be lifelong, the means an individual manages associated signs and symptoms and also connects with others can alter as well as enhance. This takes place when a person is or determines revealed, in real-time, shifts in their mood or interactive strategy and is given a chance to make various other choices that better serve them.

As a very particular technique designed to deal with concerns related to individuality and also interpersonal partnerships, TFP assumes one of these is the single or primary problems for which a person is looking for treatment. As an example, TFP may not be the appropriate initial step in psychiatric therapy for someone who also has mental health factors to consider around drug or alcohol abuse, consuming problems, or severe suicidal ideation. A person with any of these diagnoses or problems may try a corresponding treatment before beginning TFP or in correlation with TFP.

WHAT HAPPENS IN A TYPICAL TFP SESSION?

In the really starting stages of TFP, the therapist will certainly work with the private to develop educated consent. Because TFP is a unique healing method that usually utilizes a much more active technique from the therapist than other types of talk therapy, it is especially important a specific start TFP is extensively comfortable with their specialist.

There are two phases of TFP which in some cases overlap or continue to weave with each other with the program of treatment:

Establishing a trust fund, a therapy structure that will certainly assist future sessions, and boundaries that may specify to an individual's private damaging behaviors

Taking another look at the person and also exploring's mind, feeling of identification, feelings, and recurring behavioral patterns

As the private as well as specialist starts to resolve identified problems and behavioral patterns, circumstances of emotional instability, hostility, defensiveness, or other responses may emerge. Each of these events is a chance for the therapist to accentuate the psychological change or change inhabits.

This procedure of pertaining to terms with one's very own damaging idea patterns or emotional responses can be awkward or very raw-- yet most research study results related to TFP point to the effectiveness of this type of treatment. Medical trials show TFP is most effective when made use of routinely for at least one year to establish a relying on healing partnership and enough time to deal with core goals laid out early in treatment.

PROBLEMS As Well As RESTRICTIONS

The Culture of Medical Psychology prices TFP as "strong/controversial" due to blended searchings for from research studies. The majority of study indicated wonderful success connected with extended TFP treatment. Trials with doubtful results did not show TFP was inadequate-- they just raised additional inquiries concerning how much time results would certainly last or whether TFP was a clear selection over another therapy, such as schema-focused therapy.

As TFP appears to be solely put on people with borderline personality disorder, it is uncertain whether this method would work for populations without a BPD diagnosis. Extra study is needed to demonstrate the success of TFP, both for individuals with borderline as well as people with various other psychological health problems.

MENTALIZATION BASED TREATMENT (MBT).

Mentalization based therapy (MBT) is a particular sort of psychodynamically-oriented psychiatric therapy created to aid people with borderline personality disorder (BPD). Its emphasis is helping people to set apart as well as separate out their own ideas as well as sensations from those around them.

Individuals with borderline personality disorder tend to have unpredictable and also intense relationships, and might unconsciously manipulate and control others. They might discover it impossible or tough to recognize the results their actions has on other people, to place themselves in other people's footwear as well as to feel sorry for others.

Mentalization is the capability to recognize both behaviors as well as feelings and exactly how they're associated with details mindsets, not simply in ourselves, yet in others as well. It is theorized that people with borderline personality disorder (BPD) have actually a decreased capacity for mentalization. Mentalization is a component in many typical types of psychotherapy, however it is not normally the key focus of such treatment methods.

In mentalization-based therapy (MBT), the idea of mentalization is emphasized, enhanced and exercised within a supportive as well as risk-free psychiatric therapy setup. Since the technique is psychodynamic, therapy tends to be much less instruction than cognitive-behavioral methods, such as dialectical behavior therapy(DBT), another common therapy method for borderline personality disorder.

In a person with BPD, the distinction between the person's inner experience and the point of view provided by the therapist (or others), along with the person's accessory to the therapist (or others), often results in feelings of bewilderment as well as instability.

Unsurprisingly, this leads to extra, rather than less, problems in the individual's life. It has actually been suggested that people with BPD have hyperactive accessory systems as a result of their background or organic tendency, which might account for their lowered ability to mentalize. They would be specifically at risk of side-effects of psychotherapeutic treatments that trigger the attachment system.

Without activation of the accessory system, people with BPD will certainly never ever develop an ability to function in a healthy and balanced manner in the context of interpersonal partnerships.

Mentalization, like socializing or public speaking, is a skill that can be conveniently learned. People that undertake MBT will certainly discover that their treatment experience concentrates on discovering as well as practicing this skill in the context not only of their social partnerships with others, but additionally straight with their therapist.

When It's Used

MBT can be an efficient therapy for enhancing the capability to mentalize in individuals with borderline personality disorder, antisocial individuality, addiction, consuming disorders, and also clinical depression, also when various other therapies have been unsuccessful. If you lack an understanding of your various other and also very own individuals' feelings, you may have trouble both controlling your very own bothersome feelings and also habits, and also properly recognizing the thoughts and feelings of others.

What to Expect

MBT borrows usual components and strategies from psychodynamic, cognitive-behavioral, systemic, and social-ecological treatments. MBT practitioners work to develop a protected healing attachment with clients, as well as produce a risk-free environment in which people can begin to deeply explore their very own sensations as well as those of others, eventually developing their ability for mentalization. One intervention typically utilized in MBT treatment is transfer, or guiding a client's emotions towards the specialist to help with analysis of those feelings.

How It Functions

MBT assists clients to think before they react to their very own sensations or to the viewed feelings of others. With an improved capability to mentalize, individuals not only refine their very own ideas, feelings, as well as related behaviors in a different way, however also better comprehend that one more individual's ideas, sensations, and also habits might be different than the means they are analyzed by the individual. The goal of MBT is for people to not only mentalize themselves but additionally mentalize others and consider what might be driving other people's behaviors and ideas so regarding not misunderstand the definition as well as respond wrongly.

What to Search for in a Mentalization-Based Therapist

Search for a licensed, skilled mental health and wellness professional with an understanding of borderline personality disorder, as well as some training and experience in mentalization-based treatments. In addition to finding somebody with the suitable educational history and pertinent experience, search for a therapist with whom you feel comfy dealing with personal, family members, and also partnership issues.

ADDED CONSIDERATIONS

The results of these studies are encouraging, it's essential to keep in mind that much of the research study has been conducted by investigators who are evaluating their own treatments. A functional consideration is the truth that all of these psychotherapies need a significant time commitment from both clinician and person.

An additional option is the Systems Training for Psychological Predictability and also Issue Solving (STEPPS) program, created at the College of Iowa. It entails group therapy for 20 weeks, complied with by bimonthly group treatment for a year. The STEPPS program consists of cognitive behavioral strategies as well as instruction in taking care of emotions. Members of the family and also enjoyed ones are invited to join their very own sessions, in order to discover just how to react more productively to a person with BPD and to enhance lessons the person is learning in group therapy. A review recommended that STEPPS might be a practical choice to attempt when people are unable to commit to even more extensive sorts of psychiatric therapy as well as might work as an adjunct to other treatments.

TYPES OF BORDERLINE PERSONALITY DISORDER MEDICATIONS

Borderline personality disorder is sometimes treated with medications for anxiousness or depression, which have actually been shown to reduce a few of the signs and symptoms of borderline personality disorder (BPD). While there are presently no drugs authorized by the FDA to deal with BPD, they have actually been discovered to be reliable sometimes. Additionally, medications might be made use of to deal with mental conditions that often co-occur with BPD, such as significant depressive problems.

When they are utilized in conjunction with psychotherapy and also other treatments, drugs may be especially efficient for BPD. Finding out more regarding the different alternatives will help you discover the best drug option for you.

Antidepressants

While antidepressants were specifically created for people with major depressive disorder and other conditions characterized by reduced mood, several individuals with BPD are treated with these drugs.

There are numerous types of antidepressants that have been studied for use with BPD, consisting of tricyclic and also tetracyclic antidepressants, monoamine oxidase inhibitors (MAOIs), and selective serotonin reuptake preventions (SSRIs). Research study has revealed that these drugs might help with the despair, reduced mood, stress and anxiety, as well as psychological sensitivity typically experienced by individuals with BPD, but they do not appear to have a strong effect on various other signs of the problem (e.g., anger, impulsivity).

Common antidepressants consist of:

- Nardil (phenelzine).
- Prozac (fluoxetine).
- Zoloft (sertraline).
- Effexor (venlafaxine).
- Wellbutrin (bupropion).

Antipsychotics.

The term "borderline" was coined because very early psychiatrists believed that the symptoms of BPD were "on the boundary" between neurosis as well as psychosis. Because of this, some of the initial drugs checked for BPD were antipsychotics. Since this time, it has actually been located that antipsychotics can have a positive effect on a range of non-psychotic conditions, consisting of BPD. Antipsychotics have actually been revealed to lower anxiousness, paranoid thinking, anger/hostility, and also impulsivity in clients with BPD.

Common antipsychotics consist of:.

- Haldol (haloperidol).
- Zyprexa (olanzapine).
- Clozaril (clozapine).
- Seroquel (quetiapine).
- Risperdal (risperidone) (Risperdal).
- State of mind Stabilizers/Anticonvulsants.

Medicines with mood stabilizing properties, such as lithium, and also some anticonvulsant (anti-seizure) medicines, have been made use of to deal with the impulsive behavior as well as quick adjustments in feeling that are related to BPD.

There is research study to suggest that these classes of medications might be useful in BPD.

Common mood stabilizers/anticonvulsants consist of:.

- Lithobid (lithium carbonate).
- Depakote (valproate).
- Lamictal (lamotrigine).
- Tegretol or Carbatrol (carbamazepine).
- Anxiolytics (Anti-Anxiety).

Since individuals with BPD likewise commonly experience extreme stress and anxiety, medications to minimize anxiety are in some cases recommended. There is very little research study to sustain the use of anti-anxiety medication to deal with BPD.

Usual anxiolytics include:.

- Ativan (lorazepam).
- Klonopin (clonazepam).
- Xanax (alprazolam).
- Valium (diazepam).

- Buspar (buspirone).

Other Borderline Personality Disorder Medicines.

As we learn more regarding the organic reasons for BPD, new medicines are being developed and also evaluated for the condition. As an example, searchings for from one research recommend that an omega-3-fatty acid supplement can bring about decreased hostility and also feelings of hostility in individuals with BPD.

THREE HERBS SUPPLEMENT EVERYONE WITH BPD SHOULD KNOW ABOUT

There are three herbs you should know about: yerba mate, kava kava, and valerian.Please note this is all strictly my opinion: I've had luck with these herbs when the medication was not available or effective. Discuss any herb use with your psychiatrist; some herbs can interact with prescribed medications. Please also note that you should stay on your medication and use the herbs as a supplement, not a replacement.

Yerba Mate

Yerba mate is an herb from Argentina.

My friend Donna Yarema that owns a tea shop which brings yerba mate, calls this "the pleased tea" because it appears to improve consumers' moods. In fact, the store's supervisor, Randee Bennett, utilizes a yerba mate to treat her bipolar illness. Yarema told me that mate should be made like an environment-friendly tea; the water should be warmed to right before steaming, then the herb steeped to taste.

I feel like I could conquer the world when I drink yerba mate. Yerba mate is a perfect pick-me-up for when you have mild depression.

Kava kava

Frankly, this is the best anti-anxiety herb I've ever used. Pleasant was this mellow feeling that some states passed laws listing kava as an "under the influence" herb.

According to the National Center for Complementary and Alternative Medicine, kava has been shown to be beneficial for anxiety. Recommends not taking it for more than three months without consulting your doctor.

kava does not interfere with psychological alertness when considered anxiety. "Kava may be made use of rather than prescription antianxiety drugs, such as benzodiazepines and tricyclic antidepressants," the site checks out. "Kava needs to never ever be taken with these prescription drugs."

I have not had any type of issues with kava kava, but it may communicate with some psychotropic drugs. Seek advice from your psychoanalyst before making use of kava kava.

Valerian

Traditional Osage healer Lo Ha Wa Ti An Ka calls this "Grandma Planet's Valium" and also states his people utilized it as a nerve tonic. According to A Female's Guide to Vitamins, Herbs, and also Suppplements, valerian has a long custom of use in dealing with depression, insomnia, and anxiety. I utilized to use it to treat self-injury urges.

According to 20,000 Tricks of Tea, valerian was made use of in World War I-era England to deal with air assault pressure. "Sedative to the greater switchboard, valerian relieves pain, tension, as well as the effects of too much pressure to bring sleep in difficult scenarios, without morning-after results," guide reads. "It soothes the brain and quiets and also nervous system."

The book warns that valerian should not be taken with sleeping medications, since it will enhance their effects. The book notes that it's best to use valerian in small amounts in tea blends.

Those are three herbs everyone with BPD should know about. I'm just telling you what's worked for me when modern medicine either failed or wasn't available. Do your homework on these herbs or others that may help, such as hyssop, St. John's Wort or lavender.

NATURAL AND HERBAL SUPPLEMENTS FOR COMMON MENTAL DISORDERS

Numerous drugs for common mental disorders, although useful, can trigger unpleasant negative effects that discourage patients from taking their recommended dose. Over the last few years, there has been a good deal of interest in all-natural substances to treat the signs and symptoms of clinical depression, PMS and also stress and anxiety, either to improve the effects of prescription medicines or to use alone.

Research studies show that a lack of particular nutrients may add to the growth of mental illness. Significantly, essential vitamins, minerals, and also omega-3 fatty acids are typically lacking in the general populace in America and also other established nations, and are incredibly deficient in people dealing with mental disorders.

Lots of experts believe that nutrition has the prospective to affect the signs and symptoms and extent of anxiety. Supplements consisting of omega-3 fats, vitamins C and E, and also folate have been checked out.

Omega-3 fats such as eicosapentaenoic acid (EPA) and also docosahexaenoic acid (DHA) may have an impact on clinical depression because these substances are widespread in mind. The proof is not completely conclusive, yet omega-3 supplements are an alternative. One to 2 grams of omega-3 fatty acids day-to-day is the typically accepted dosage for healthy people, however, for patients with mental illness, approximately three grams have actually been revealed to be efficient and also safe.

Supplements that contain amino acids have actually been discovered to lower symptoms, possibly since they are transformed to natural chemicals in the mind that help alleviate anxiety. Serotonin is made using the amino acid tryptophan. Nutritional supplements that contain tyrosine or phenylalanine, later on exchanged dopamine as well as norepinephrine, are also readily available.

Deficiencies of magnesium as well as the B vitamin folate have actually been connected to clinical depression. Tests recommend that clients treated with 0.8 mg of folic acid each day or 0.4 mg of vitamin B12 daily will certainly have decreased anxiety symptoms. Clients treated with 125 to 300mg of magnesium with each dish and at going to bed have actually revealed quick healing from significant clinical depression.

Specialists have checked out a series of organic treatments and supplements for individuals with anxiety. The evidence supports the effectiveness of kava for mild to modest anxiousness conditions. Kava does, nevertheless, effect on other medications metabolized by the liver.

St John's wort, valerian, Sympathy (a mixture of The golden state poppy, hawthorn as well as important magnesium) and passionflower have actually been explored for anxiousness yet the research studies have actually generally been small or irregular. Lower than typical omega-3 levels have been reported in clients with anxiety, and also supplementation with omega-3s shows up to enhance some symptoms. Zinc and also chromium supplements might be useful, along with calcium and vitamin B6.

Tests of ladies with premenstrual syndrome (PMS) suggest that vitamin B6 "relieves total premenstrual and also depressive premenstrual signs and symptoms." Dietary research studies likewise indicate that calcium taken at 1,200 mg per day may work.

Four hundred IU per day of vitamin E has actually revealed some effectiveness, as well as a number of various other supplements are under investigation. These consist of manganese, tryptophan as well as magnesium.

Calcium supplements are one more appealing alternative. Variations in calcium degrees may help clarify some functions of PMS. Exhaustion, hunger changes, as well as depressive symptoms were substantially boosted in one study of females receiving calcium, compared to sugar pill.

People with obsessive compulsive condition (OCD) usually take advantage of selective serotonin reuptake inhibitors (SSRIs), so the nutrients that increase serotonin levels are likely to reduce signs. Again, the amino acid tryptophan is a precursor to serotonin, and tryptophan supplements can increase serotonin degrees and treat OCD.

St. John's Wort has actually also been shown to profit OCD signs. A dosage of 900mg per day of St. John's Wort has actually been found to enhance OCD signs and is less most likely to create negative effects, but it can disrupt some prescription medicines.

There is incredible resistance from clinicians to making use of supplements as therapies, mostly as a result of their absence of understanding of the topic. Others rather use prescription medicines that the medicine companies and the FDA researches, monitors and also remember if needed.

" Nevertheless, for some patients, prescription medications do not have the effectiveness of dietary supplements as well as they often have far more harmful side effects. For clinicians to prevent these supplement treatments since of an absence of understanding and objection to make use of therapies not backed by medication business as well as the FDA, they are endangering their patients' recovery."

Psychoanalysts should be aware of nutritional therapies, suitable dosages, as well as feasible adverse effects in order to provide alternate and corresponding therapies for their people. This may minimize the number of noncompliant patients experiencing a mental illness that choose not to take their prescribed drugs.

Why Alcohol Isn't The Answer to Borderline

Reason 1: It Makes Borderline Symptoms Worse

Lots of people use alcohol to self-medicate a psychological problem such as borderline personality disorder-- I'm one of them. It's so usual that compound misuse is a sign and symptom of BPD. While alcohol is originally satisfying, it inevitably brings the individual utilizing it down.

In my active addiction, I consumed alcohol to obtain intoxicated. I consumed alcohol to elevate my state of mind and also consumed alcohol once more to stay on that fabricated high.

I wandered all over downtown, determined to locate an open bar or an open liquor shop. When I couldn't discover one, I cursed my luck. "I'm sober!"

Alcohol additionally raised my symptoms of psychosis. The voices often reprimanded me for getting drunk, so I consumed alcohol more to close them up. If that really did not work-- and also it rarely did-- I would self-injure to shut them up. When it made them worse, which was most of the time, I would certainly call for help. This usually led to a medical facility remain, where I would certainly dry out, remain sober for concerning a month, after that regression.

Since I'm sober, the self-harm, the voices, and the hospital stays are a great deal much less frequent. I comprehend that if I don't handle my addiction, I won't be able to manage my psychiatric signs. Alcohol is my enemy.

Reason 2: Alcohol Interferes with Borderline Medication

Alcohol is a depressant-- after the intoxication wears off, you collapse. It terminates out the antidepressants one might be taking.

One more reason it hinders the medication is that alcohol is a diuretic. When alcohol consumption, you generate some really pricey pee. In that urine is your medication-- you are not allowing your body time to metabolize it, and therefore not enabling your body time to use it to treat your trouble.

Since I'm sober, my drugs have a chance to function. I'm not cancelling them out or doing away with them before they have a chance to work. Consequently, my BPD signs and symptoms remain in check. And also as long as I'm sober, they have a possibility of remaining this way.

One of my friends on the twin diagnosis device at Richmond State Hospital described alcohol as "my lousy lover." That's precisely what it is. It exists to you when it claims it's your pal.

Reason 3: Alcohol Limits Your Inhibitions

Alcohol has fueled many an "I was so drunk I ______" tale. It is popular for limiting your inhibitions-- inhibitions such as, "Don't attack that large tattooed individual called Bruno," or, a bit closer to home, "Don't reduce on your own" and "Remember to take your medication."

One evening I was waiting for the bus when a drunk guy came up to me and also began touching me. The alcohol had actually eroded his judgment to absolutely nothing. He had no restraints, and also due to the fact that of that got a cost-free journey to jail.

Now imagine mixing that absence of restraints with the impulsiveness common in BPD. Currently you know why alcohol-fueled so many healthcare facility keeps.

Alcohol is not a response.

Addiction

Addiction is a psychological and physical failure to stop eating a chemical, compound, task, or medication, even though it is causing emotional and also physical injury.

The term addiction does not just refer to dependency on compounds such as heroin or cocaine. An individual that can not stop taking a particular medication or chemical has a material reliance.

Some dependencies also entail a failure to stop taking part in tasks, such as betting, eating, or functioning. In these conditions, an individual has a behavior addiction.

Addiction is a persistent disease that can additionally arise from taking medications. The overuse of suggested opioid pain relievers, for instance, triggers 115 deaths daily in the United States.

When a person experiences addiction, they can not control just how they use a substance or partake in an activity, and also they come to be depending on it to cope with day-to-day live.

Yearly, addiction to alcohol, cigarette, illegal medicines, and prescription opioids costs the U.S. economic climate upward of $740 billion in therapy costs, shed job, and also the impacts of criminal offense.

Many people begin utilizing a medication or initial take part in a task voluntarily. Nevertheless, addiction can take control of and also decrease self-constraint.

DEPENDENCY VS. MISUSE

Medicine addiction and also drug misuse are various.

Misuse refers to the incorrect, extreme, or non-therapeutic use of body- as well as mind-altering substances.

Nevertheless, not everyone that mistreats a substance has an addiction. Dependency is the long-lasting failure to modest or cease intake.

As an example, a person who consumes alcohol heavily on a night out may experience both the blissful and also damaging impacts of the compound.

Nevertheless, this does not certify as an addiction until the individual really feels the requirement to consume this amount of alcohol on a regular basis, alone, or sometimes of the day when the alcohol will likely impair normal tasks, such as in the morning.

An individual who has not yet developed an addiction may be avoided more usage by the harmful side effects of substance abuse. Waking or vomiting up with a hangover after consuming alcohol also much alcohol may hinder some people from consuming that amount anytime soon.

Someone with an addiction will remain to misuse the substance even with the damaging results.

SIGNS AND SYMPTOMS

The main indicators of addiction are:

uncontrollably seeking medicines

frantically taking part in harmful degrees of habit-forming behavior

overlooking or shedding rate of interest in activities that do not involve the dangerous substance or habits

connection problems, which usually entail lashing out at people who determine the reliance an inability to quit utilizing a drug, though it may be triggering health issue or personal troubles, such as concerns with work or partnerships

hiding habits or substances and or else exercising privacy, for instance, by refusing to discuss injuries that occurred while drunk

profound modifications in look, including a visible desertion of hygiene

raised risk-taking, both to access the substance or activity as well as while utilizing it or taking part in it

WITHDRAWAL

When a person has a dependency, and they quit taking the substance or involving in the habits, they might experience specific symptoms.

These signs consist of:

anxiousness

irritability

tremors and trembling

nausea or vomiting

throwing up

exhaustion

an anorexia nervosa

If a person has actually regularly utilized alcohol or benzodiazepines, as well as they stop instantly or without clinical supervision, withdrawal can be deadly.

TREATMENTS

Medicinal advances and also development in identifying have actually aided the medical community to establish different ways to handle and solve addiction.

Methods include:

behavioral therapy and also counseling

medication and also drug-based treatment

medical tools to deal with withdrawal

dealing with associated emotional variables, such as anxiety ongoing like reduce the threat of relapse

Addiction treatment is very customized and also usually needs the assistance of the person's community or family members.

Therapy can take a long time as well as might be made complex. Addiction is a persistent condition with a variety of mental and physical results. Each compound or action may call for different management.

NOTE

Addiction is a major, persistent dependency on a compound or task. The occurrence of dependency sets you back the U.S. economic climate thousands of billions of dollars each year.

A person with a dependency is incapable of quitting engaging or taking a compound in actions, though it has unsafe impacts on daily living.

Misuse is different from dependency. Compound misuse does not always lead to addiction, while addiction entails regular misuse of substances or involvement in hazardous actions.

Signs and symptoms of dependency frequently include decreasing physical health, irritability, exhaustion, and a lack of ability to stop engaging or utilizing a substance in actions. Addiction can cause habits that strain connections and prevents day-to-day tasks.

Ceasing to make use of the substance or involve in the behavior often causes withdrawal signs and symptoms, including queasiness as well as trembling. Do not try to instantly stop using alcohol or benzodiazepines without medical guidance.

Dependency therapy can be hard, yet it is effective. The very best kind of treatment relies on the compound and also the discussion of the dependency, which varies from one person to another. However, treatment often entails drug, counseling, and area assistance.

THE THREE BIGGEST LIES ADDICTION TELLS

Addiction can be one of the symptoms of borderline personality disorder. In my instance, alcoholism both gas as well as is sustained by my psychological conditions. As I've progressed in treatment, I've discovered that every little thing dependency informed me is a lie.

Addiction Lie # 1: Sobriety is Terrible

This resulted in an addict's worst worry: I ran out. I failed to remember that it is unlawful to sell alcohol on Christmas Day in Indiana as well as strayed all around midtown Indianapolis browsing for alcohol.

That understanding was my initial indication that I was vulnerable over alcohol and that my life had actually come to be uncontrollable. A few months later, I checked myself right into rehab and also have not had a drink given that.

In my energetic addiction, I dreaded soberness. I thought that alcohol was self-medicating, and to some level it is, yet at the finest it concealed my signs and symptoms and also at worst made them even worse. Ever before given that ending up being sober last year, I've observed that the voices are gone.

Soberness is a wonderful thing that just those that have it understand. I can truly say I'm grateful to be sober, if only because my psychiatric signs are in check.

Addiction Lie # 2: I can stop at any time I Want To; I simply Don't Want To

Chances are great you're addicted to whatever it is you think you can quit if you've ever before stated this. Attempt quitting and also see exactly how badly you want the compound-- if you need to have it, if you can not live without it, you're addicted. As the joke goes, "If I can consume alcohol like a typical person I would certainly consume alcohol constantly."

In my energetic addiction, I commonly said this. I didn't desire to stop, yet I did want to stop. I wanted to stop, yet the truth was I could not.

If you can go without it for a day, ask yourself. If you can't, possibilities are you're addicted. Look at your life outside the dependency-- if you have no outdoors life as well as your life focuses on using the substance and also getting in question, you're addicted. If you don't intend to quit, chances are you're addicted. Acknowledging the dependency is the very first step towards recovery.

Addiction # 3: I'm Functioning; it's not a Problem

In Alcoholic's Anonymous (AA) we call this "a situation of the yets," and it's an insidious lie for lots of people with substance abuse trouble. I haven't shed a task-- yet. I haven't been detained--. When we compare our chemical abuse to the DSM-IV criteria, we might locate ourselves thinking, "That hasn't taken place." It's important to add the word "yet.".

A mental health expert when informed me that considering that I was functioning, my alcoholism wasn't a problem. She was wrong. In fact, at the time I was seeing her on an emergency basis as a result of an alcohol-fuelled self-destructive state.

While I never lost work or obtained arrested due to my alcoholism, there are times when I should have lost work or been arrested. While I managed, essentially, to stay out of difficulty while an intoxicated university student, there were indicators that something was wrong. It was obvious to everyone except me that despite the fact that I was working, it was a great mystery regarding how.

Be cautious of the yets.

Adjustment the Stinking Thinking.

These three lies mark an addicted state, however they're only 3 instances of lie-based thinking that substance abuse or substance dependence motivate. To recoup, you have to quit listening to the lies. You have to change, you're having an odor thinking. As we claim in AA, it is less complicated to act on your own into a new way of assuming than it is to assume on your own right into a new method of acting. Go through the movements sufficient as well as you'll discover that they become your way of life. When you offer it a chance, the fact has an amusing means of thriving.

WHEN DOES DRUG EXPERIMENTATION BECOME DRUG ADDICTION?

Due to the fact that cannabis is not authorized for clinical use in Indiana, that evidently makes me a cannabis addict.

It makes me question: When does drug experimentation ended up being drug addiction?

When You Can't Stop Using a Drug

The initial time I used cannabis was when I was recuperating from a surgical procedure. I also comprehended how somebody could become addicted.

One cautioning indicator of medication addiction is you can't quit making use of the medicine. If you have to have it, if there's no such thing as enough, if you keep making use of in spite of negative consequences, after that your trial and error has come to be an addiction.

Apply the list of symptoms of alcohol addiction to your utilizing pattern if you're unsure; I favor the CAGE test (Cutting Back, Annoyance, Guilt, Eye-Opener). HealthyPlace.com has a medication misuse evaluating the examination. If you have a problem, these examinations are a great way to identify.

Testing becomes an addiction when the compound in question is the most vital thing in the world. Medicine experimentation becomes an addiction when your life focuses on getting and also utilizing the substance in question.

When You Use the Drug to Treat Symptoms of Mental Illness

I made use of marijuana for the 2nd time when I was attempting to eliminate off a psychotic episode. Long story short, it really did not work as well as my friends took me to the psych ward. There is a relationship between psychosis and also marijuana usage, but it's unclear if those influenced use marijuana because they're psychotic or if they're psychotic due to the fact that they utilize cannabis. Yet it does not matter-- when you're using a substance to deal with a mental disorder, you've got the risk of crossing over from trial and error to addiction.

I utilized alcohol to treat my borderline symptoms, not recognizing that it made those symptoms even worse simply as frequently as it made them much better. If this defines your material use, your experimentation has ended up being dependency.

When You Wonder If You Have a Problem with Drugs

Your testing has most likely become an addiction if it obtains to this point. That said, you're most likely the last individual to understand you have a problem.

When asked me if I would certainly think about going to Alcoholic's Anonymous, my college specialist. I responded that it had not been that negative, as well as she countered that she thought it was. I remained in rejection for the rest of the year, but at some point understood that she was right I did have trouble.

I understood several other times that I had trouble with medications, too. When I feared going out, I understood I had a problem. I recognized I had an issue when I roamed around midtown Indianapolis looking for a bar that was open on Christmas Day due to the fact that I required a beverage. When I was eliminated that my court dedication really did not consist of a ban on alcohol, I recognized I had an issue. When I recognized my stopping factor was when I might no more feel my face, I understood I had an issue.

What do we do? One therapist informed my family that if drug addicts aren't most likely to meetings, they're utilizing

(I differ given that I remained sober for three years without going to conferences). Acknowledging the issue is the initial step to resolving it. We should do even more than simply recognize the problem-- we have to take action. Whether that's a 12-Step program, rehabilitation or outpatient treatment, we have to do something.

Even if testing becomes an addiction, there is hope we can stop.

BPD & RELATIONSHIPS

Personality disorders are a distinct group worldwide of mental disorder. While somebody with anxiety or anxiousness might feel that they are experiencing signs that are various from their normal state, individuals with personality disorders usually stop working to realize that their emotions and also responses depart from the regular human experience. People with borderline personality disorder (BPD) battle to comprehend exactly how partners, husbands, pals, and various other family members experience their extreme reactions, mood swings, and risky actions.

Needless to say, if you have an enjoyed one with BPD, life can be filled with dilemmas and also disputes. You could seem like you're being held hostage, stressing that your family members will certainly harm themselves if you do not appease them. You might question whether you must let them obtain cash once again or respond to the loads of voicemails they left on your phone. Handling borderline personality disorder requires skills for deescalating situations and also fostering independence in your loved one. With the right devices and area techniques, it is possible to aid your loved one towards recuperation.

Signs and Symptoms

Just a medical professional or psychological health expert can formally offer an official diagnosis of a personality disorder, yet there are numerous key symptoms you can observe that may suggest an individual has BPD. These include:

- Intense fear of being rejected, separation, or abandonment
- Rapid changes in between thinking somebody is excellent to believing they profane
- Risky actions consisting of risky sex, gaming, drug use, or gathering charge card financial debt
- Threats of self-destruction or self-harm
- Difficulty feeling sorry for other individuals
- Mood swings from ecstasy to extreme shame or self-criticism
- Frequently losing one's mood

The Effect of BPD Symptoms on Intimacy

The resource psychological health and wellness experts describe when making a diagnosis, signs of BPD include extreme, unstable, and clashed personal connections.

Fundamentally, people with BPD are typically frightened that others will certainly leave them. Nonetheless, they can also move all of a sudden to feel smothered and scared of affection, which leads them to take out from relationships. The result is a constant back-and-forth between demands for love or attention and also sudden withdrawal or isolation.

Another BPD symptom that particularly affects partnerships is called desertion sensitivity. This can lead those with BPD to be regularly looking for signs that someone might leave them and also to translate also a small event as an indicator that abandonment looms. The feelings may cause frenzied initiatives to stay clear of abandonment, such as begging, public scenes, and even literally avoiding the various other people from leaving.

An additional usual issue of liked ones in borderline relationships is lying. While existing and deception is not part of the official diagnostic standards for BPD, lots of liked ones claim existing is one of their greatest issues; this can be since BPD triggers people to see points really in different ways than others.

Spontaneous sexuality is one more traditional sign and symptom of BPD, and many people with BPD battle with concerns of sexuality. Likewise, a large percentage of individuals with BPD experienced childhood sexual abuse, which can make sex extremely made complex.

Various other symptoms of BPD, consisting of impulsivity, self-harm, and also dissociative signs and symptoms, which can have an indirect impact on borderline connections.

If a liked one with BPD is involving in impulsive actions like going on investing sprees, it can create major anxiety within the family. Furthermore, self-destructive gestures can be scary for enchanting partners and also can present great deals of stress and anxiety into the connection.

What Research Says About BPD and also Romantic Relationships

Study has verified that people with BPD often tend to have extremely rainy charming connections characterized by a great deal of tumult and dysfunction. One research study demonstrated that ladies with BPD signs and symptoms reported higher chronic relationship tension and also more constant conflicts. A lot more severe an individual's BPD symptoms are the much less contentment their partner reports.

Additionally, research study has additionally revealed that BPD symptoms are connected with a majority of romantic connections in time, and also a greater occurrence of unexpected maternities in women. Individuals with BPD likewise often tend to have even more previous partners and also have a tendency to terminate even more connections in their social media networks than people without personality disorders. This suggests that romantic connections with individuals with BPD are more probable to finish in a breakup.

Finally, in regards to sex, research has actually shown that ladies with BPD have extra lack of confidences regarding sex, are most likely to really feel forced right into having sex with their partner, as well as are extra ambivalent regarding sex than ladies without BPD Little research study has actually been done on sexuality in men with BPD.

Starting a Romantic Relationship With Someone Who Has BPD.

Provided all the problems that exist in BPD relationships, why would anybody start a connection with somebody with the condition? It's vital to keep in mind that regardless of these intense and also turbulent signs and symptoms, people with BPD are regularly great, kind, as well as caring individuals. Frequently they have many positive qualities that can make them fantastic enchanting companions some of the moment.

Lots of people that have been in a romantic connection with a person with BPD talk regarding just how fun, amazing, and enthusiastic a BPD companion can be.

Can You Make a Romantic BPD Relationship Last?

Many BPD connections experience a honeymoon period. Individuals with BPD will certainly usually report that at the beginning of a new romantic relationship they put their new companion "on a pedestal" as well as in some cases feel they have actually found their best match, a true love that will certainly save them from their psychological discomfort. This kind of thinking is called "idealization.".

This honeymoon duration can be extremely exciting for the new companion also. After all, it's actually nice to have a person feel so highly concerning you and to feel as if you are required.

When a person with BPD realizes that her new companion is not perfect, that image of the ideal (idyllic) heart mate can come crashing down. Due to the fact that people with BPD battle with dichotomous reasoning, or seeing points only in black as well as white, they can have problem identifying the fact that a lot of people make mistakes even when they indicate well.

The secret to maintaining a partnership with somebody with BPD is to locate means to manage these cycles and also to encourage your BPD companion to get specialist assistance to reduce these cycles. Often companions in BPD relationships are helped by pairs therapy.

Just how should I structure the house atmosphere?

People with BPD take advantage of a home environment that is calm and relaxed. All entailed relatives (including a boyfriend or sweetheart) ought to know not to review crucial concerns when the individual remains in dilemma setting. Stop to take a breath on your own when they do become emotionally responsive. It's also vital to not center all discussions around the condition and troubles. Alternatively, it's vital not to put too much focus or praise on progress, or a person might begin to self-sabotage. Individuals with BPD must have possibilities to talk about their passions as well as thoughts regarding the information, family members occasions, and various other pastimes. Make an effort to poke fun at an amusing joke or eat dinner together numerous times a week. The much less a specific feels like his/her mental disease is under the spotlight, the more possibility they need to discover various other elements of themselves.

Exactly how can I communicate successfully throughout a crisis?

When a loved one comes to be reactive, they might come to be to disrespect you or make unfair allegations. You have to remind yourself that an individual with BPD has a hard time to put themselves in various individual's viewpoints.

Instead, when they come to be reactive, make an effort to pay attention without pointing out the imperfections in their argument. Try not to take it personally. If the individual does explain something you can have or improve done wrong, recognize their factor, apologize, and also suggest a way you can improve on the issue in the future. If the private seems like they're being listened to, the crisis is less most likely to escalate. If the conflict climbs to the level where an individual is throwing a full-on outburst or endangering you, it's ideal for walking away as well as resume the discussion when they are calmer.

What happens if they threaten to injure themselves?

If a person with BPD starts to intimidate to damage themselves, a dilemma is escalating. In some cases self-harm indicators might be less obvious, such as scraping the skin, consuming less, tinting or cutting off hair, or isolating from others. These activities stand for the person's inability to express their emotions vocally. Recognizing very early indicators can aid protect against an emotional situation from becoming more serious or needing psychological or clinical attention.

Instead, you welcome the specific to talk concerning their feelings and permit yourself to gauge whether expert help is required. That does not suggest you have to call 911 every time specific talks concerning harming themselves. Instead, ask your family members what they would really feel most comfy doing when they endanger injury.

What various other approaches can minimize disputes?

Reflecting as well as paying attention can be the most effective strategy in communicating with a person with BPD. It merely recognizes an individual's feelings and perspective.

Statements of reflection and also summing up can also aid a specific feel listened to. It's concerning assisting your family members in feeling heard and de-escalating the problem.

What can I do when I feel overwhelmed?

Since a household participant with BPD might not be able to offer compassion and also self-awareness required for a partnership, it's important to have various other assistance in your life. If you require to chat concerning the experience of living with someone with a psychological health problem, support groups, mental wellness professionals, spiritual leaders, and also your physician can be superb sources. No solitary individual must be liable for connecting comfortably and reacting to situation circumstances.

Will they ever entirely recover?

Unlike with physical disease, healing has a different significance when it comes to mental wellness. Healing does not indicate the total elimination of signs, the lack of requirement for medication or therapy, and also operating similar to individuals without the condition.

Handling a Romantic Relationship Involving BPD.

Along with pairs therapy, for the individual with BPD, there are therapies that have been revealed to be effective in terms of aiding with partnerships:

Dialectal Behavior Therapy (DBT): DBT is a type of cognitive-behavioral therapy that associates an individual believes in their actions. There are 4 main abilities taught in DBT, and among them is taking care of interpersonal skills.

Mentalization Therapy (MBT): MBT is a therapy that focuses on helping somebody make sense of what is taking place in their mind and the minds of others.

Medications: There are presently no medications accepted to deal with BPD, yet they are in some cases suggested by doctors to aid enhance specific symptoms of borderline personality disorder. Study recommends that specific medications can aid an individual handle their clinical depression, impulsivity, and also anger. On that note, however, it's vital to consider thoroughly the negative effects of medicine with its possible benefit.

Ending a BPD Relationship

Several concerns might arise when a BPD partnership is ending. A separation can leave them feeling absolutely desperate and devastated since people with BPD have an intense anxiety of abandonment. Even if a connection is undesirable, an individual with BPD can frequently have problem allowing the relationship go. This is particularly real of long-term collaborations or marriages.

This is why it's a great suggestion to have a support network for you and also partner, particularly if a separation may occur, as well as this network often includes a mental health expert.

NOTE

On a favorable and also final note, please bear in mind that the diagnosis for BPD is great. This suggests that while lots of people with BPD do experience recurring signs also after time and also treatment, in the long-term there is frequently really hope that your relationship with your liked one can work.

BPD AND YOUR SEX LIFE

Borderline personality disorder (BPD) signs and symptoms can affect your emotional state, your relationships, and also your ability to regulate your behavior. It's not shocking that BPD can likewise have a significant impact on your sex life. While very few scientists have examined BPD and also its impacts on sexuality, more and more job is suggesting that individuals with BPD can experience numerous essential difficulties with sex.

Mindsets About Sex

Study has actually demonstrated that females with BPD often tend to have more unfavorable attitudes concerning sex. Ladies with BPD report having a better number of blended feelings about sex-related relations, and are also a lot more most likely to feel pressured to have sex with their sex-related partners.

There may be a variety of factors for these more lack of confidence toward sex. Initially, numerous women with BPD are survivors of kid misuse, which might contribute to overall unfavorable reactions to adult sexual experiences. Women with BPD are extra likely to experience a terrific offer of problem in their partnerships, so they may feel much less positive regarding sex.

Reckless Sex

Impulsive habits are just one of the symptoms of BPD noted in the DSM-IV. When it comes to sexuality, a fad towards spontaneous behavior may lead to reckless sex-related behavior too.

People with BPD are most in danger of taking part in impulsive acts when they are experiencing extreme psychological reactions, or when they are disinhibited by alcohol or other substances. Intense despair, fear, jealousy or positive feelings may additionally result in impulsive sexuality.

Indiscrimination

In addition to engaging in negligent or impulsive sex, there is evidence that people with BPD are extra susceptible to sexually promiscuity. This differs from impulsive sex because indiscrimination is the act of purposefully having several sexual companions (instead of having casual sex on an impulse).

Why might people with BPD be a lot more promiscuous? One opportunity is that they make use of sex to deal with feelings of emptiness that are connected with the problem. When feeling vacant, numb, lonely, or burnt out, sex might generate positive psychological feedbacks.

Evasion of Sex

While some research studies have shown a boost in sex-related actions in individuals with BPD, there is additional evidence that some really stay clear of sex. For instance, in a 2003 research, Dr. Mary Zanarini as well as associates found that people with BPD reported avoidance of sex for anxiety of experiencing an exacerbation of their signs and symptoms.

Your Sex Life

While the study is much from definitive (as well as is specifically sporadic with regard to men with BPD), there is proof to recommend that individuals with BPD can experience a range of sex-related difficulties. It is likely that the impact of BPD signs and symptoms on sex can differ considerably from person to person, and can take extremely various types. Just how your symptoms impact your sex life may necessitate some reflection or perhaps a discussion with your specialist or partner.

THINGS PEOPLE WITH BPD WANT YOU TO KNOW

Borderline personality disorder (BPD) is a mental disease noted by an ongoing pattern of varying moods, self-image and also behavior." Therefore, those with BPD often act impulsively, have unstable partnerships and experience episodes of anxiousness, anger as well as anxiety.

But to those who have not experienced the weight of BPD either within themselves or a loved one, this description may not suggest much to you. Below are some points we want you to find out about BPD:

We Feel Too Much

According to Marsha Linehan, a designer of dialectal behavior treatment (DBT), people with BPD are mentally sensitive from birth. This amazing level of sensitivity makes individuals with BPD to really feel emotions on a better and also a lot more extreme degree than the norm.

As a result of This, Our Love For You May Reach Heights You've Never Experienced

When we succumb to a person or something, we fall hard. The emotional side of our brains-- the side that commonly overtakes us without our approval-- ends up being the facility of our emphasis. Relationships with us can be extreme beyond belief, with the notion of love enveloping you with every praise and also inspiration we give. We want you to grow and do well into the outstanding human being we believe as well as feel you are, and we have no trouble in all doing whatever it takes to show you that.

We Can Sometimes Be Cold And Distant

Do they love us sufficient? Even individuals who feel too much can train themselves to feel nothing at all. People with BPD are incredibly delicate as well as will certainly do whatever it takes to avoid this extreme feeling of real or viewed abandonment.

We Don't Mean To Send Mixed Signals

I've been in situations with my friends as well as a member of the family where I've idyllic as well as devalued them many times in my mind I've lost count. And that's frequently only in the period of a few hours! We want so severely to reveal others just how much we enjoy as well as value them, yet our fear of abandonment makes it difficult to do so without transforming our minds 24/7. Even a regarded mild can sometimes make us question whether we must stick the relationship out in the future. If we can not even understand our own emotions, I picture its none less complicated for another person.

The Emptiness Can Often Be Too Overwhelming

Individuals with BPD are recognized to be really impulsive. The root reason for this is important, too. One of the many symptoms of BPD is persistent sensations of vacuum. This isn't your average 10 mins of monotony since you're really feeling weary or careless. No, this is a consistent feeling of pure openings within that leaves you starving for any type of sense of significance, any kind of sense of direction via the seemingly pointless insides of our minds. We wish to do something, anything for it to vanish. This frequently consists of spontaneous, negligent and also self-destructive habits.

Sometimes We Scare Ourselves (A Lot).

Originally, this extreme form of mental disorder was considered on the borderline between psychosis and also neurosis, which is why it is now coined "borderline personality disorder." While BPD has a focus on emotional dysregulation, a number of us also experience devastating forms of psychosis, consisting of delusions, hallucinations and hefty disassociation. Disassociation is one of the trademarks of BPD. Envision sensation so overwhelmed with emotions and exterior stimuli that you no longer really feel grounded in your very own globe-- as if you have been secured from the truth as well as are currently analyzing on your own from an outside point of view in order to escape difficult scenarios.

Our Past Traumas Play More Of A Role Than We Realize.

Research studies on BPD have shown environmental influences contribute to the growth of BPD. Such impacts include youth forget, abuse, distress and also maturing with a relative with severe mental disease. When distressing events are present during early youth, healthy and balanced development can become stunted and cause issues in later life. This might likewise cause retaining child-like habits such as black and white thinking, absence of item durability and also psychological dysregulation. We might not recognize (or intend to comprehend) the effect our childhood years might have in our grown-up lives, yet it deserves trying to heal those open wounds and identify the roles they play in our BPD.

Comorbidities Are Our Best Friends.

A study cited on the National Institutes of Health states that "individuals with a BPD diagnosis are likely to have countless co-occurring physical comorbidities and psychological disorders." The most usual comorbidities including: anxiety, bipolar illness, anxiousness condition, rest condition and also material used condition.

We Are Trying Our Best.

We wish to get better, believe me. We do not want to allow our feelings, self-confidence and also past traumas to determine individuals we are and will become. We want to enjoy you for who you are, not disconnect every single time we feel somebody slowly slipping away. Whether with DBT, medication, self-awareness or all the above, we are attempting our finest.

The Love And Patience You Give Us Mean More To Us Than We Can Ever Express.

While we realize we are fighting with an extreme mental disease, we usually contemplate just how much we appreciate those that linger as well as love us regardless of our struggles. The love as well as perseverance you provide us means the globe to us, particularly in times where we doubt whether we really deserve it.

THE EMOTIONAL VULNERABILITY OF BORDERLINE PERSONALITY DISORDER

Much so that every time you merely touch the location, it's like the injury rips open again, and also once again, and again; and also the pain peaks every solitary time. Currently picture this injury represents your psychological sensitivity as well as how you deal with the globe every day. This is akin to the emotional vulnerability of borderline personality problems (BPD).

Manning cites one intriguing research where scientists tickled babies on their noses with a feather. Their actions ranged extensively: Some infants really did not respond at all, others walked around and still others began sobbing as well as it was tough to relax them down. These children were seen as "conscious psychological stimulations."

Like various other conditions, BPD also includes an environmental component. (Not every person who's mentally sensitive takes place to have BPD.) Individuals with BPD aren't simply genetically at risk of feelings; they've also matured in an "invalidating setting." So they might've never ever discovered how to manage their feelings, or their emotions were continually disregarded or dismissed.

What It Means To Be "Emotional".

According to Manning, being emotional isn't an absence of control; it has more to do with "3 different tendencies that cause emotional stimulation in different means." These are:.

" Emotional Sensitivity." When someone with BPD has a psychological response relatively out of nowhere, loved ones aren't the only ones confused. Individuals with BPD might be uninformed of the trigger, as well. Yet they still have a strong reaction. "Emotional sensitivity wires people to respond to hints as well as to react to their reactions." Manning describes that: "To understand emotional level of sensitivity, consider the person with BPD as being 'raw.' His emotional nerve endings are subjected, therefore he is really affected by anything emotional.".

Manning factors out that psychological reactivity isn't manipulative or self-indulgent, which is an unfortunate misconception attached to BPD. Instead, research has suggested that individuals with BPD have a higher psychological baseline. If the majority of individuals' emotional standard is 20 on a 0 to 100 scale, after that people with BPD are constantly at 80.

"In a person with typical psychological intensity, an emotion fires in the brain for around 12 secs. There is evidence that in people with BPD emotions fire for 20 percent longer.".

REAL-LIFE STORIES OF BPD SURVIVOR

This is an open letter to anyone ready and/or requiring to pay attention. I am 26 years of ages, I reside in Wichita, KS, and also I live with my daddy due to the fact that I can not live alone. Presently, my BPD signs are aggravating.

I was identified with BPD about 7 years earlier. I went residence and also investigated every little thing I might regarding it when I was told what it was. I was delighted because all of my troubles lastly had an explanation, and also just perhaps I had not been such a bad person. Possibly it had not been all my mistake like I was constantly informed and also I constantly thought. And most notably, perhaps I had an opportunity to improve.

Individuals started informing me that I was using my diagnosis as a reason for my bad habits. It's like every action I had actually ever taken to much better myself because of my medical diagnosis, just never took place. As well as it felt like absolutely nothing I can ever do to try to improve myself would ever matter to the individuals I cared for, due to the fact that of every little thing that had actually happened in my past.

A lot of my family doesn't believe in my medical diagnosis, and any friend I ever made has left due to the short amount of times when I could not regulate my feelings. I could never blame them for not wanting to be around me, yet this all left and leaves me with definitely no support system. Yes, I live in my dad's house, yet we barely talk, as well as I harbor so my temper toward him that in some cases I can't talk with him due to the fact that I don't recognize what awful words can appear of my mouth. My surroundings have left me seeming like there is no hope, due to the fact that no person intends to aid. Not someone like me. Not a person with suspicious actions in their past.

I check out The Art of Asking by my preferred artist Amanda Palmer, and it was definitely wonderful. That publication made me see that there are great people in the world. That some people actually are prepared as well as even excited to assist, and that makes me smile every damn time. I need constant pointers of this, because if I do not it seems like I will certainly lose faith in humankind entirely, which will certainly shatter every idea I have ever before held dear. I want there to be love on the planet. I wish to know that mankind can be stunning. I would like to know that honesty as well as loyalty exist. I need them to ... however as a derelict to culture, I don't see it. My belief in it is fading.

The intensity with which you really felt those feelings is most likely equal to what a person with BPD feels on a regular basis. Your mind, your body, are entirely taken over as well as you finish up doing something you regret deeply however have to live with. People will certainly tell you that whatever you did was your mistake, as well as you will certainly believe it, however they don't and can not comprehend just how tough you dealt with to keep control.

It can easily finish up feeling hopeless and also you feel helpless. Your lack of emotional control leads you to damage your connections, leading individuals to stroll away from it, which worsens the desertion concerns that are a component of your disorder. I absolutely think that I will certainly never ever get better, because I am bordered by unfavorable people with unfavorable sensations towards me that I then reciprocate toward them.

Yesterday, I had to say goodbye to a dear friend of mine, since I ended up being emotional and said points I never ever need to have. I attempted to be liable. I walked away so she would not have to manage that; since no one ought to need to. I told my brother or sisters what I truly considered them a couple of days prior to that, because they always use my past versus me, and also lie concerning me. As well as a pair days ago I put my guitar away and said, "I'm done."

I simply wish more people were mindful of how destructive the points they say really are to any individual with any kind of mental health problem. The even more individuals are conscious and also care, the even more individuals we can assist. I may feel hopeless, yet I don't want other individuals too.

I understand there is a shift in the center of this brief description of my experience from speaking to individuals with mental illness, toward speaking with those without it. Originally, I had intended for those without it to review as well as hopefully get just a grain of understanding. Yet that will only take place if others that share in the experience find this and share it with others. My intent was to explain the trouble while staying short.

CONCLUSION

Borderline Personality Disorder (BPD) is an emotional problem a human person could possibly have identified frequently by extreme mood swings, the trouble of keeping partnerships as well as reduced self-confidence. Psychologists could not find any type of solid proof for its cause yet however they have this finding that it could most probably originate from the injury experienced during one's youth. It could be in the form of kid abuse, abandonment or the loss of a close loved one.

Specialists are being prevented from doing treatments to individuals that have this sort of disorder under the age of 18. This is since psychotherapists think that the personality of one is still in the process of establishing, as a result, it would be tough for them and also for the patient to deal with this sort of condition.

The means to heal or moderate Borderline Personality Disorder, according to some psychotherapists, is for the person having this condition to have a solid support system that is fully knowledgeable about this type of abnormality and treatment that would really aid the person to overcome this sort of condition.

Support system must be completely familiar with the tendencies the person has for them to recognize what he/she is going through. Due to the fact that if his/her family members do not recognize how to deal with the disorder, propensity will be, problems would actually develop which would absolutely beat their objective of sustaining.

If this will not aid one learn how to deal with the abnormality he/she has, therapies will be worthless. These need to strengthen everyone having Borderline Personality Disorder in order for the individual to have the ability to stop patterns in the following generational cycle from duplicating.

Do Not Go Yet; One Last Thing To Do
If you enjoyed this book or found it useful I'd be very grateful if you'd post a short review on Amazon. Your assistance actually does make a distinction and also I read all the reviews personally so I can get your feedback and make this book even better.

Thanks again for your support!